The Love That Saved Me

JULIUS L BAKER

LifeRich Publishing is a registered trademark of
The Reader's Digest Association, Inc.

This book is a work of non-fiction. Unless otherwise noted, the author
and the publisher make no explicit guarantees as to the accuracy of
the information contained in this book and in some cases, names of
people and places have been altered to protect their privacy.

LifeRich Publishing books may be ordered through booksellers or by contacting:

LifeRich Publishing
1663 Liberty Drive
Bloomington, IN 47403
www.liferichpublishing.com
844-686-9607

Because of the dynamic nature of the Internet, any web addresses or
links contained in this book may have changed since publication and
may no longer be valid. The views expressed in this work are solely those
of the author and do not necessarily reflect the views of the publisher,
and the publisher hereby disclaims any responsibility for them.

Any people depicted in stock imagery provided by Getty Images are
models, and such images are being used for illustrative purposes only.
Certain stock imagery © Getty Images.

Scripture taken from the King James Version of the Bible.

ISBN: 978-1-4897-3006-0 (sc)
ISBN: 978-1-4897-3007-7 (e)

Print information available on the last page.

LifeRich Publishing rev. date: 12/29/2021

Contents

Introduction

I pray that this book will be a blessing to all that are going through. I pray that this book will be a blessing to you. If God brought me through what He did, He is able to do the same for you. He will see you through it. His love is real even in the midst of it. To experience the Love of God and to know that He is there. You can make it on the other side of the storm. May God bless you and keep you.

Dedication

This book is dedicated to my wife Diana Baker, the wonderful woman in the world. She is my inspiration. God has truly blessed me the most amazing wife. I praise God for her prayers and her encouragement. The bible says when a man findeth a wife he findeth a good thing I ambles to have this woman of God in my life.

CHAPTER ONE

Love in the House

I was born in St. Augustine Florida, great family and at that time, my father was a Deacon in the church before he became the pastor. Many good times growing up. In the home, we would all get in the car, go to church, and have good time. In the Lord, I was raise up in a large family, five boys and five girls. In a four bedroom and one bath home, we did not have much, but there is a whole lot of love in the house. My mother was a praying woman and she loves us. A great cook. She looked after us the way she loves us. The love of a mother sent us to school, taught me how to cook and to pray. She really loves the Lord in just how she loves us. Her love went all the way. My father went to work and saw that we were provided for and got ready to go to church. My father said something to me when I was growing up. He said, "Son, well manners and respect will take you places where money can't take". I did not understand then, but when I got older, I understood when I was 18.

My mother pass away to go be with Lord. That was a tough time in my life. Oh how I miss her. But time heals all wounds, but the love of God brought me through. I never forgot how she love us and the love of God was operating through her that when sat down to eat she would feed other kids to through. I was beginning to know the love of God and just how real His Love is.

My father became pastor of the same church and been pastoring there now for over fifty years. He had an open-heart surgery and still going strong and how he loves my mother. A good man work hard. I learn a lot from him. He instills in me how to be good to your wife, to love her like Christ love the church. Things I have seen God brought him through. I remember he had a brown truck that was the only transportation we had and someone stole it and drove it out on the beach into the salt water. He would get us ready and we would walk to church. Not too long after that, he got another truck. No matter what keep the faith in God my father is a man of faith. He raised us with love. Wept us when we needed it. Gave us chores to do and we had to have them done before he got home. But he has a love for us, I am truly blessing to have been raised by such a great father and to carry on what he instills in me.

We all have storms in our lives. The most important thing is getting through those storms. There are short storms and long storms, but the key to it is to keep the faith. He will put no more on you than you can bare. When there's love in the house when one hun the whole family hun. The family comes together and help the one in need no matter what situation was. We were there for each other. Remember when I was a little boy, I accidently drink some kerosene. My mother grab me quickly and got me to the hospital. Her love for came to my rescue after coming from the hospital, I was fine.

LOVE RESCUE

When love is in the house, the atmosphere is sweet. There is happiness and joy. I remember awhile back we had one of those old time washing machine with the wranger on top of the machine. The wranger had two rollers that you put the clothes through to wrang the water out of the clothes. Clothes was washing that day, I tried to put the clothes through the wranger. I was a little boy at the time and my hand got caught it he mists of those two rollers my hand went through started up my arm I began to yell for my mother. She came and rescued me and got me out of the wranger. I had a broken arm but I was saved that's why Jesus came God love us so that He sent His son to save us to rescue us from a life of sin. When I yell my mother heard my cry and came running to me. God does the same. He listens for our cry. My ear is not heavy that I cannot hear you neither. My hand too short that I can't save you when think that no one loves you. God does. He loves you. If you ate homing He loves you that's what held Him to the Eros, just my mother came to my rescue. God will do the same for you whatever the case may be knowing He's just a prayer away. He is listening to our cry.

UNCONDITIONAL LOVE

Love - A feeling of warm precolonial attachment that what we had in the home no matter how much we argue, fuss fight, we still had love in the in the home. I remember one Christmas I didn't have any money but I wanted to get my mother something for Christmas. I made her a bowl made of popsicle sticks and painted it blue I wrap it up and she open it. The look she had on her face like if she opens a present with a million dollars in it. I made it with love no matter how bad we were at times, our parents love us unconditionally.

Unconditionally - not limited by any conditions. Their love for us was not limited. They love us all the same that the same way that God loves us unconditionally no matter how we had live, God yet loves us. He loves us to send His only begotten son to die for the sins of the world or if you have habit that you can break, God still loves you. He is able to take that habit away from you.

ABIDING LOVE

Abide- To take up one's abode to reside to be prepared able to endure love. Live in our home I find out that love comes from where it abides. When love is in the love is going to come from that home because love was given to us unconditionally.

LOVE WITHOUT DOORS

There's need to be an opening for love to come through when the doors are close love can't come through. When we can let the love of God flow in our lives and keep the doors open for His love to operate in our lives other will come to want to know that love that you have. You loving Him and you loving Him oh what a feeling is to be loved by Him.

CHAPTER TWO

Love in the Mist of a Storm

Love in the midst of a storm. There are all kinds of storms in life. There are some to get your tension. There are some that comes to try destroy you. And there are some that comes to stop you, and there are some that comes to make you afraid. We had storms growing up in the house but the love of God brought us through those tough times. When love is in the midst of the storm you got protection shelter in St. MARK the 5th chapter 35-41.

And the same day when the even was come, He said unto them let us pass over unto the other side. And when they had sent away the multitude they took him even as he was in the ship and there were also with him other little ships. And there arose a great storm of wind and the waves beat into the ship so that it was now full. And he was in the hinder part of the ship asleep on a pillow and they awake him and say unto him. Master carest thou not that we perish. And he arose and rebuked the wind and said unto the sea, "Please be still and the wind ceased and there was a great calm. He said unto them, "Why are you so fearful? How is it that ye have no faith?" And they feared exceedingly and said one to another what manner of man is this that even the wind and the sea obey Him.

They had love in the midst of that storm. When you are in the midst of a storm, God don't want you to fear. He wants us to have faith in storm. God always knows what we go through before we get to it, but He is always there. One of His promises is that never to leave us nor forsake us. Love is always there on board. In the next chapter I will begin to tell you about a storm that I been through. All true nothing fiction. Every detail that happen is true. What I went through, what had happened to me, but through it all God is with me and may He be with you.

LOVE IN THE HEART

Romans the 5th chapter verse 5 says, "And hope maketh not ashamed because the love of God is shed abroad in our in our hearts by the Holy Ghost which is given to us. Even that go through the storm God wants us to still have love in our heart, to love him as we go through it and He is always there to hear our call. Through His love we can love our enemies and love the way He loves. His love is perfect."

SECURITY IN THE STORM

2 Thessalonians 3:5, "And the Lord direct your hearts into the love of God and into the patient waiting for Christ. There is security in love protection His love will protect you from the back of your enemies". His love will give you protection in the storm even when lied on false accuse. His love is close by when Moses was a baby and pharaoh put out an order that the male baby's to be put to death. Moses' mother got a basket pitch it inside out and put Moses in it and down the Nile River Moses went. God protected Moses as he went down the river. There are crocodiles that swim in that river. Through the danger of your storm protection is there for you. Sometime in the midst of a storm the heat of the storm can be so tense that it seems hard to bear like that you feel that if you don't know if you are going to make it. The Hebrew boy's wain the burning fire furnace the heat

form it was to sever the mighty men died from it God protected them from the heat. They came out unharmed. God will do the same thing for you. His love will bring you out unharmed.

LOVE WITHOUT FEAR

Ment 1ˢᵗ John 4:18-21, "There is no fear in love but perfect love cast out fear because hath torment He the feareth is not made perfect in love, we love him because he first loved us. If a man say I love God and hateth his brother. He is a liar for he that loveth not his brother whom he hath seen how can he love God whom he hath not seen. And this commandment have we from him that he who loveth God love his brother also". As you can see God does not want us to fear His love is perfect it's the work of the enemy to get you to fear tell the enemy I will not fear it's something God did not give you the spirit of fear for God hath not given us the spirit of fear but of power and of love and of a sound mind. You can fear is not of God, but He have given us power love and a sound mind when we face our storm do not fear, go through, God is there every step of the way. David face a lion and a bear he did not fear.

JOY IN THE STORM

JOY - gladness of the heart, as you going through that's something that the enemy want to rob you off there's a song that say out all I've been through I still have joy. There is another song that says this joy I have the world didn't give it and the world can't take it away. Joy is everlasting! Therefore, the redeemed of the Lord shall return and come with singing unto Zion and everlasting joy shall obtain gladness and joy and sorrow and mourning shall flee away. The joy of the Lord is everlasting.

Joy is weeping for His anger endureth but a moment in his favor is life weeping may endure for a night but joy cometh in the morning tears of joy sometimes you cry when you are going through but tears of joy. I can understand that when going through you cry but I will get into all that the next chapter what happen in m y life but I still have joy I spent a lot of nights weeping but I had to hold on. I knew morning was coming but through the midst of it all the joy of the Lord is my strength.

1st Psalm 18:6 - And it came to pass as they came when David was return from the slaughter of the Philistine that the woman came out of all the cities of Israel singing and dancing with cabarets with joy and instruments of music praise as you go through the storm give God praise Him any way it may hurt in the storm praise HIM to the rising of the sun to the going down the same His name is to be praise yes praise your way through it.

FAITH IN THE STORM

Faith - confidence in the testimony of another. Rev II: I - Now faith is the substance of thing. Hope for the evidence of things not seen there was a story once told that a man name John and John love color greens and his wife was cooking him some he thought that he would come for lunch and get some greens his wife said they're not done yet so he got 2 slices of bread and put on top of the lid of the greens and the smell of those greens got into the bread. John wrap them in foil and went back to work his coworkers say John got some greens. John said no all I have is the substance of the greens we don't see how you going to make it through but keep the faith in the Lord. He will see you through it all the just walk by faith not by sight. We go through it with faith in God. Luke 17:5 - And the apostle said unto the Lord, increase our faith if you are low in faith God will increase your Faith.

STAYING FOCUS

Focus as a camera lens or the eye the bibles says the disciple were on a boat and they look they saw a man walking on the water they thought it was a spirit but when he got close Jesus said be not afraid it is I Peter say Lord if that you bid me to come and Jesus said come Peter got off the boat and walk on the water and when the waves got high and the wind blowing he took his eyes off of Jesus and looked at the wind and began to sink and Peter said Lord save me and Jesus reach and saved him. Peter took his eyes off of Jesus stay focus on JESUS he is the one that's going to see us through. He is in control of the situation storms can be tense especially when you are in the middle of it but the key is do not doubt GOD keep the Faith in Him.

PRAYING IN THE STORM

Praying is an important thing to men ought to always pray and not faint sometimes it takes all night prayer Matt 6:6, But thou when thou prayest enter into thy closet and when thou hast shut thy door pray to thy Father Which is in secret and thy Father which is in secret and thy Father which seeth in secret shall reward thee openly there was a song I've heard that keep on praying, God is neigh just keep on praying. He will hear your cry for the Lord has promise He will answer you through prayer you can bounce back from the storm. Pray when you feel like it. Pray when you don't feel like it. Prayer is the key faith unlocks the door. The Bible declares and says for us to come boldly to the throne of grace men ought always pray and not faint. You gain great strength through prayer. Prayer and praise is a great thing to do when going through. When the disciples were on the boat in the midst of a dangerous storm Jesus was on board asleep when they awaken Him and said master careth not that we praise He rebuke the wind and the water. It obeyed him that is the authority that is in his words its power in the word of God by faith they could have spoken to the wind and water by faith it would have obeyed them the same authority is in the believer to speak to the atmosphere. We serve the almighty God that have all power in His hands. A God that is able to do anything but fail now unto Him that is able to do exceeding abundantly above all that we ask or think according to the power.

ASKING IN PRAYER

Prayer- The act of asking for a favor with earnestness petition. The Bible says with prayer and thanksgiving let your request be known to God. There is an old song that says just a little talk with Jesus will make it alright. The fire is burning the prayer wheel turning just a talk with Jesus make it alright. In Christ name St. John 14:13-14 - And whatsoever ye shall ask in my name thy will I do that the Father may be glorified in the son. If ye shall ask any thing in my name I will do it in the midst of the storm asking God in prayer in His name in faith it shall be done. The name of Jesus carries power in that demons got flee. In the word of God it says in Matt 7:7, "Ask and it be given seek and ye shall find, knock and the door shall open", ask seek and knock the key thing in prayer along with faith in Matt 20:21-22 Jesus answered and said unto them verily I say unto you if ye have faith and doubt not ye shall not only do this which is done to the fig tree but also if ye shall say unto this mountain be thou removed and be thou cast into the sea it shall be done And all things whatsoever ye shall ask in prayer believing ye shall receive you can depend upon the word of Jesus stand up on His word and His promises His promises is ye and amen. The word gives you the strength that you need stay in the word in and out of a stone everything is going down but the word of God. His word is the solid foundation. We can stand on faith in His word gives all that we need to get through the storm there is no secret what God can do what He done for other He do for you.

UNITY IN PRAYER

Be bound in heaven and whatsoever ye shall loose on earth shall be loose in heaven again I say unto you that if two of you shall agree on earth as touching anything that they shall ask it shall be done for them of my Father is heaven for where two or three are gathered together in my name there am I in the midst of them. Where there is unity there is strength. It's good to have a prayer partner someone to help pray you through the storm one can put a thousand to flight not that you can't pray alone his good to have that prayer partner that there for you and not against you someone that's going to stand with you in faith when the two of you agreeing together Jesus said that He would do it not by power not by might but by my Spirit says the Lord God moves on faith. Faith causes Him to move on your petition in Heb. 11:6 says, "But without faith it is impossible to please him for he that cometh to God must believe that he is and that he is and that he is a reward of them that diligently seek him when we seek Him whole heartedly He will reward you seeking Him in faith.

EXPECTATION

St. Mark 11:24, Therefore I say unto you what things so ever ye desire when ye pray believe that ye receive them and ye shall have them knowing that God already got it done faith says it done each day that goes by you know that God is going to do it.

THE POSTURE OF PRAYER

Standing - Neb- 9:5
Kneeling - Ezra- 9:5
Sitting – 1 Chr.- 17:16-27
Bowing - Ex.-34:8

STAND

When you done did all you can stand in EPH.6:20; finally, my brethren be strong in the Lord and in the power of his might. Put on the whole armor of God that ye may be able to stand against the wiles of the devils. For we wrestle not against flesh and blood but against principalities against powers against the rulers of the darkness of this world against spiritual wickedness in high places. Therefore, take unto you the whole armor of God that ye may be able to within and in the evil day and having done all to stand. Stand therefore having your loins girl about with truth and having on the breastplate of righteousness. And your feet shod with the preparation of the gospel of peace. Above all taking the shield of Faith where with ye shall be able to quench all the fiery darts of the wicked and take the helmet of salvation and the sword of the spirit which is the word of God. Praying always with all prayer and supplication in the spirit and watching thereunto with all perseverance and supplication for all saints. And for me that utterance may be given unto me that I may open my mouth boldly to make know the mystery of the gospel for which I am an ambassador in bonds that therein I may speak boldly as ought to speak. Stand strong in the storm stand dress for ware in the storm in your war gear ready there are battle that belongs to the Lord but the thing is here is to stand in this scripture is to tell us how to stand we stand in the power of God's might.

Stay in God's Word

Read your bible every day stay in the word of God it's food to our soul it's life is solid it's powerful it's sharper than any two edge sword. In storm that you go through it's in the word that we can read that will help us make it to the other side of the storm.

CHAPTER THREE

The Storm of Life

Before I get to the storm that I been through and how the love of God saves me His love been with me through the whole thing if had not been for the Lord that was with me I don't know what would had happened to me it could have been worse than it was this was a storm like no other that I been through with but I held on to God and He held to me hold on to God I am still holding on to God and get close to Him as possible rely 100% on God. He says in His word greater is He that's in you than he that in the world when you have the greater on the inside I had to rely on that a whole lot God's word I had to stand on it as I said in previous chapter the storm that I been through is a storm like no other I would not wish this on worse enemy but the love of God was always there for me one of His promise is that never to leave me or forsake me it's all God that gave me victory by His power there is an old song that says victory shall be mine if I hold my peace and let the Lord fight my battle victory shall be mine God get the glory for all I been throughI truly can tell you that God is an awesome God. He is amazing. In relying on GOD'S word it is life and power in His word. His word is a lamp to my feet His word guided me through me through the storm step by step it was hard tough damaging but God brought me out of that storm in the bible in 2 Cor. 10:3-5 for though we walk in the flesh we walk in the flesh we do not war after the flesh. For the weapons of our warfare are not carnal but mighty through God to the pulling down of strong holds. Casting down imaginations and everything that exalted itself against the knowledge of God and bringing into captivity every thought to the obedience of Christ. Yes, I depended on God and His word in is it says no weapon form against me shall prosper Gal. 2:20 I am crucified with Christ nevertheless I live yet not I but Christ liveth in me and the life I now live in the flesh I live by the faith of the Son of God who loved me and gave himself for me. God and his word is top priority in my God is first in my life his word and prayer these are the things that's very much needed in the storm.

The storm that I went through is call witchcraft the storm that would have taken me out but the love of God was with me through the whole thing step by step. Thing that happen is unbelievable but it all true nothing fiction all that I'm about to tell is all true you will know just how real His Love is. The spirits that was use at me are real those was sent at me God is in control of the whole. You may feel the vibes of the storm but God is in control relax God is in control there was time when I said God where are you those was that I felt like I was alone but wasn't He was there to shield and protect me it all started when the Lord told me to stop going to this specific house I obeyed the Lord and the work began the water heater went out at the house have to take a bath the old time way where that you would heat water on the stove and pour the water in the wash tub stand in it to take a bath but before that I went to this mothers house to cook and cooked them a mother day dinner these three individuals was working together all along there was also a dog being use in this as well so I cooking behind my back something was place in the food the main one that was in charge was running back and forth to their bedroom the second one went to the third party to get what was needed to start their plan prior to this one ask the other what will I do there was I won't going to do anything when the food was ready sometime. Stuff like this comes from who you least expect I never would have thought that it would have come from these three but it did so after the dinner I notice something was not right I began to feel strange in a way that was not normal when I got to the house a bath was taken and that was stuff place in the water I was ask to pour the water out and when I did immediately they ran to their chant after pour the water out I stood in front of the kitchen sink and I saned to like if I was being peel like a banana I was trying to gain control of my thought like strength was strip of me allow me to say this here I was told this that I have not seen the tip of the ice burg of they was going to do to me and they was 100% right this is just the beginning of it I have not yet scratch the surface yet all of this was going on in the house where I was living but through it all God got me as I get for there in to this they wanted to take me out but God said not so I learn something in this that is to be obedient to God that a big key to it He got the power to keep you they wanted to control me to do whatever they wanted to do to me but God was with all the way. They worked hard to weaken me down to triumphed over me God will show you things I dream I was looking out my bedroom I seen four wooden soda crate each one had the head of a snake the head of a cobra one to the top was giving orders to the other three telling them what to do I began to pray talk to God who was the ones that got the snake heads the enemies I wanted to know who they were and sure enough God showed me who they were as I kept going through the back of the my feet kept feeling like they was being squeeze I really was feeling this my mind was being blocked that I could not think clearly it was like they wanted to do as they command they sent spirit leach on to me to speak using the sound of my. My voice and I have not said anything it was so bad that even things were put out on the internet about me you will be surprised just how evil peoples can be. So many folks were misinformed about me. Having peoples thinking you are crazy when you are not. On this particular night I was sleeping and all out of the clear blue sky I was pounce on like a lion on his prey then I woke up, I was shocked in disbelief that this woman would do this to me for days. I just thinking why, what have I done to be done like this. She yields her to it I went to another room of the house and I went to the doctor. The hall way was dress with a smell that was about to take my breath and ran out of the house in order to breath. On the next day I was laying on the floor praying and the Lord spoke to me and said get up and go look up under your side of the bed and I did. I looked and was in open bible so I got it and throw it in the river. I question her about it. The statement was I quote trying to put the word in me when you accept Jesus a Lord and Savior you got the Word in you Jesus is the word as John said the word was made flesh so there was no way you put them in any body that way I praise God for being as awesome as He is in the book of psalms many of the aphiliction of the righteous but God deliver them out of them all there's a whole lot to tell about the storm I been through a God told the Apostle Paul that my grace is sufficient for you many of the Apostle and the prophets went through a lot of things but God was always there He will be there for you.

CHAPTER FOUR

In the Storm

When you are in the storm and trouble is on every side, I know by self-experience that it can be rough. Many things going through your mind, then you have to pull your mind together. Thank on the word of God, His word will help you make it through it. Getting back to the storm that I been through, I remember that the head one that in charge says to me, to your house I want to but I didn't do it, but the daughter brought her there to work her evil. As time went on, I began to find different thing up under sofa pillows still wondering why, what have I done, but I realize the mother was not going to be let down. Then there was a pulling spirit being use at me. I was going through so much. Mind being block trying to think clearly so even in my sleep I was attack with weird types of dreams. I'm very thankful that God is a good God. Through it all I learn to trust in Jesus and to trust in God and to depend on His word. I would go outside and sit down and think, so when I moved to the other house we serve a mighty good God. One day, the Lord spoke to me and said go on a 7-day fast drink nothing but water and cranberry juice. I obeyed the Lord and did it and when I came off that fast God showed me something as clear as crystal. I've seen in a vision that I was standing in this house I looked at the wall. I've seen the thermostat on it. I looked down the hall at the end of this hall way was a door that kept opening and closing. Remember I ask God who it was then the door open all the way and the person on the other side came out. I knew who they were and I saw what they were wearing. About one week later, I was sitting in the car. The same person came wearing the same thing. I've seen them wearing in the vison. God gave confirmation on what he showed me, there is still much to tell about this that I've been through I been through so much to tell about what had taken place in my life. After my clothes was dress with a substance I will feel like a gathering around feet's and legs the spirit of heaviness been sent at me. When I get up I would feel the weight like if I was giving someone a piggy back ride then I began to quote Isiah put on the garment of praise for the spirit of heaviness it will get off me how great is our God.

My legs and feet got filled with fluid and blister came up on my legs. It was so bad that it would seep out and there would be a puddle of fluid on the floor. The hallway floor was dress for me to walk on and I would not be sleepy they would send a sleeping spirit that I would go into a hard sleep. There was a time that I would have to fight to shake it off and I would see demonic spirit that sent at me. I would see them circling around. I went to the doctor that I would have to get my feet and legs wrap up to my knees. By going to the doctor I develop a disease called mercer. This disease can kill you. I had to go into the hospital with IV in my arm and they had put a sprint in my arm that went to my head. I was quarantined. I got fevers up to 100 degrees but God was right there. I had to be on a strong antibiotic. It was so bad that I had to leave the hospital and go to a nursing home. While I was in the nursing home having prayer every morning, the Lord showed me something. I laid there in bed and I looked in my house and seen the 2nd person and the niece dressing the recliner that I sit in. I was able to look from the outside in, looked and see the evil that was going on in the house. Can you imagine how that was to see that as time went by I get out of the nursing home and still praying. Then one day my life was out of control.

I wasn't praying or reading my bible. I have even isolated myself, stayed to myself day after day. I was attacked by demonic force, but glory be to God He never left me. Then one day he spoke it was time to leave and I call my sister about can come and stay she says yes that Sunday. I pack up left and if not been for the love of my Lord and Savior Jesus Christ thing would be worse than that, but for the Lord is on my side there. I have to start all over again with everything. It doesn't feel good going through the storm but coming out of the storm when you can see the light at the end of the tunnel. I had to wait on God wait on the Lord and be of good courage and He shall strengthen your heart. Worst part of a hurricane is the eye of the storm where it is the most dangerous part of the storm. I been through some heated part of this storm. It blew at me, I had to get grip and to pull myself together to bounce back from this. Thinking positive thought and being positive, I'm glad that we serve a God that will never leave you or forsake you. He was there all the way. The sun will shine after the storm. When a storm is over, then the aftermath of the storm is picking yourself up.

CHAPTER FIVE

Picking Your Self Up

Picking up after a storm is a job I have seen where that when they would go through things trying to salvage whatever they can. Then things be turn down in order to rebuild with better material. Storms in life happens for a reason. God is in control to give you greater and better than what you had. In cleaning up after the storm, thing be all out of order this be there that be somewhere else they go through their stuff looking and sometimes wondering where to go from here. There is one person that knows His name is Jesus. He knows where you would go from there. He knows where you are going, what avenues to travel and what roads to cross. Keep your hands in picking yourself up after the storm. The bible declares and says in Philippians 3:13-14, Brethren I count not myself to have apprehend but this one thing I do forgetting those thing which are behind me and reaching forth unto those things which are before I pray toward the mark for the prize of the high calling in Christ Jesus forgetting those thing. Meaning not to even think about it like it never even happen to you but the trick of the enemy is to try to keep you in mind of it to oppress you with it bringing it up to you forgetting it is our job and press forward to the high call in Christ Jesus in moving forward you began to move into your future one thing that I came to know my ending is going to be greater than my beginning the word of God is my starting place but greater is He than in me then He that's in the world God is greater then what ever you may face God is bigger than the situation you may be going through there is power in His blood pleading His blood against the enemy the blood that will never lose its power protection is in the blood the storm that happen in my life to know how God just did not allow them to destroy me but still I came out with the victory the whole time my mind was made up that I'm going to serve God no matter what God is my all and all that why I love Him so much with all my heart strength and with all my might.

As Jesus said forgive them in which I did I forgave them to move on as Jesus taught the disciple to pray in going through the storm at one point I was told to drink some Pepsi Cola soda and ammonia but I did not do it God took care of me in this thank God for His word God is my strong tower He is my shelter in the time of a storm I will talk about it in a lower chapter on how the Lord bless me with the wife I have now when He bless me with Diana He gave me greater God is good in picking up after the storm getting myself together starting over I was staying to my sister house when I started writing this book praying and writing on how the Lord brought me through His love is so amazing his grace and most of all His joy the joy of the Lord is my strength as I sat and write the Lord showed many of things many of nights I would go into all night prayer through His love He began to put my life together again even though I had to come out of isolation the love of GOD in all of that things are going to be greater in my life the anointing the calling on my life the love of God in picking myself up His love this love you could not find in a store nor a mall you can find this love in God no greater love then this He laid down His life for us all through the hurt the pain His love was there for me through the storm His love brought me out of that storm delivered from that evil that was done to me they meant it for evil but GOD turn it for my good I had to learn not to complain about what been through nor through a pay party the blessing thing is that I was still able to hold my head up the storm I did no wrong and nothing to nobody looking straight ahead to the end of the storm many of days I had do like David encourage myself I had a lot of hard and tough days while hell was coming at me in all direction I held on to God I told myself that you're going to make it through this God got purpose and a plane we go through things sometimes we go through for someone else All things work together for the good those that love the Lord who are called according to Hiss purpose as said about a pity party don't help but a praise party you don't need any music I will bless the LORD at all time and His praise shall continue be in my mouth His name is to be praise to the raising of the sun to the going down the same his name is to be praise. PRAISE THE LORD.

In that what I went through was thy wanted to control me I came to realize that there are people in the world that are that evil to go to a level where God want to carry you. You will go through something I been through some things to get to where God is carrying me I made it through darkness the rain through pain but I made it the bible says in everything give thanks it didn't matter what I was feeling I had to give God praise oh the song say my soul looks back and wonder how I got over when I came through this it was nobody but the Lord that brought me through it the pain I felt no aspirin could cure it if it could I would have gotten cases of it there was time I felt I was alone like God where are you and then I was not alone the words of Jesus I am with you nor forsake you there. There are many of dark days I looked wondering when was the break of day was going to come they attack my mind so they thought I was going to be lock away in a multinational place but God kept my mind He said not so we serve an awesome God you Have to keep your mind on Jesus He said in His word that He will keep you in perfect peace it don't matter what kind of storm it is it's what you do while you are in the storm as we have said don\ have a pity party there is a Reason you're going through it you will have people laugh at you storm is Enough itself and talk about you behind your back and make fun of you But through all of that God is saying I'm here for you it was very tough for me but the blood of Jesus that flows from inner veins that loose me from all my guilt and stain the reaches to the highest mountain the blood that flow to the lowest valley the blood that gives me strength from day to day it will Never lose its power I stand because of God standing in the power of his Might Christ paid the price for when He died on the cross when it was over with I can see clearly with peace in my mind my spirit and in my soul He will surround you with songs of deliverance in picking myself up through His love I found out His strength is made perfect in our weakness in The bible it declares and said cast all you cares on Him for he cares for you it's good to have a prayer partner the fervent prayer of a righteous man avail the much newer what cast it on the Lord He cares when you think that no one cares God does God will perfect that which concerneth you He knows how to handle yours and mine situation He knows just what to do He don't need a blue print on how to fix it.

CHAPTER SIX

The Power of His Love

The love that save me from all of this is a love with strong protection and go all the way with you His love never runs out and never gets low there is power in His love that how you can love your enemies through His love His love covers a multitude of sin it's the love of God been there for me through the hurt and pain His love was right there through my tears.

Those were days that I cried because of the pain David said I cried to the Lord and He heard my cry His love will never leave you to hold you care for you low save my life is love for me and His love save me from them trying to control me His love save me from my mind being attack it's an old saying that says what goes around comes around or better yet when you dance to the music you got to pay the piper I had to hold on to GOD unchanging hand not some of those days was tough for me it was tense it was times that I felt like giving up but I would be encourage to hold on mainly because of what God had promise His promises are real and a men I knew that He going to bless me when I felt low His love will pick me up I knew I was safe in His arm I didn't talk to many people about it some would not understand His love made me strong His love will never give up on you people will give up on you but the love of God never give up on you many of times when I was going to be delivered many of I found myself saying

Lord how long how long but the power of His love would give me the peace that I needed to carry on and make it with my head held up I found out that jealousy is will cause people to do you harm it almost cause David his life when those woman started to sing Saul kill his thousand and David his ten thousand the bible said that Saul eyed David and took a javelin and threw it at David and missing him it stuck in the wall it is a driver it drives people to kill do wicked stuff destroy a person good name you don't have to have a lot of stuff for folks to be jealous of you it can be the call and the anointing that God got on your life.

The power of His love is a weapon the weapons of our warfare is not conal but mighty through God to the pulling down of strong holds love your enemies do to those that don't like you pray for those that despiteful use you but through it all I would mind my own business folks will get mad at you or you have peace and they don't have none I was up against a lot of different kind of spirits and seen many different kinds from alligator to possess to Skunk to sneaks black sneaks to cobras to rattle snakes as you can see why the Lord is with me I had no fear for the Lord is on my side but the power of the love of God protected me there was a constant work trying to weigh me down the power of the love of God kept me up I was not standing on my strength but on the strength of God they even have me surrounded by their work but the bible said whom the son had made free is free indeed.

Stand therefore in the liberty where that Christ has made me free the power of the love of God made me free as I sat there and wrote at my sister house way before I move to Daytona all of this happen before I move to the city of Daytona writing about the pass of what the love of God brought me through oh to have the power of God's love to bring you out of something like that is a mighty work of God His power is all mighty by His right hand He gave me the victory I praise God for the gospel songs that I listened to. That help me those are the songs that help me make it to the next level they are also the songs that help me through the rough heated part and the power of God with His mighty right hand oh last and see that the Lord is good for His mercy endures forever I'm not going under but I'm going over the love of God is a powerful thing when God is you have to depend on theirs is a song they use to sing when I was a boy Lord fight my battle He knows how to fight the battle vengeance is mine saith the Lord I will repay from that I learn how to really stand on God's word and His promise His word is a lamp to the path way of my feet the power of His love will lead you all the way through the storm meditate on his word day and night and He will make your way prosperous and also be of good courage be not afraid as God was with Moses and He is with me even when I was surrounded by the evil work but the power of God's love is in me and around me the power of His love will outshine any darkness that may be around you and me so let us walk in the power of His love.

On that day when the Lord brought out of the evil work of witchcraft in 2012 on what was a feeling that was on that day I can now become all what God wants me to be get to where He wanted me to go the power of His love delivered me I step out to step in to the blessing of God the power of God it was a fight but God won the battle being like that the it was with me like that the power of God's love prepared me for future things to come in ministry and in other as I said before this just one of the blessing of God I will talk about later in another chapter how He has bless me with the most amazing good wife a man can have the woman that this book is dedicated to Diana my wife for life a real woman of God. The power of God love is standing power to help you stand in the storm to give you everything that you need to make it you can be as low as you can go the power of His love pick you up from that place to another the power of His love is mighty when the children of Israel was at the red sea and God cause an east wind to blow and the Red Sea open up for them to cross the same God will open up your Red Sea for you to cross on dry land you can shout and give God praise that you made it when what was done at me God had His hand on me and took care of me through the whole ordeal and show how great

His power is I came out unharmed no damage the power of His love He brought the Hebrew boys out of a furnace unhurt unburn and the same God brought me out the same way when you go through the storm and the Power of His love eyes have not seen ears have not heard the good things that God have in store for those that love Him even that I went through I love God with all my heart my strength and my might I never left Him because I know that He will never leave me the power of that love He loves the unlovable but now we know that He loves us but we got to love Him back it's not a one way thing He's loving but there is no return love oh how I love Jesus because He first love me while we was yet in our sins He died for us yes the power of that love broke the chains of the enemy off me the power of that remove the residual of every work that was done to and at me the Power of His love nothing can penetrate it the power of that love is genuine power of His love will always be there never to leave the power of that love will carried me many of days we draw strength from the power of that love.

CHAPTER SEVEN

Holding on to His Love

Holding on to God no matter what you will have some strong storms in life the wind of storms is strong the winds of a hurricane is very damaging the more wind it picks up the more dangerous it is they goes up into categories 1 2 3 or 4 and even 5 I have where it have peel the shingles off roofs break windows tear houses businesses and so on I have seen where that news reporters be talking in the news trying to stand in the storm and the wind of the be about to blow them away they looking for something or someone to hold on to I remember living in the Kissimmee Florida and a Tornado came I was told that a young man and his wife and child was in the house he got his family in a closet when he got them in there the wind from the tornado reap through the house and he tried to hold on but the wind pull him away from his family he have not been seen or found to this day.

In holding on in a storm you got to hold on to something solid something that will not give way something that will not uproot itself because of the wind holding on through it when the Apostle Paul was on a ship and a storm came on the sea the wind from that storm was so strong that it tore the ship in pieces that he told everyone to grab a board from the torn ship and hold on and float to shore I want to encourage you can make it even you to make it on broken pieces to bring you through it Job had to hold on after losing his children his cattles sores covered his body his wife telling him to us his God and die his friend saying you must have sin that's why you going through this you don't have to do any wrong to go through a storm it not good too bad about some because they going through it's alright with you today you don't where you be to tomorrow but the main thing is that Job held on and said I'm going to wait to my change come that one thing that encourage me I knew it was not going to be like this always that's something about a storm it will not be a storm always many time God will send help to you to make it through the storm you hold on a change will come the thing is God still in control of the storm no matter what it look like or what it feels like God is still in control of the storm hold on to Him and He will hold on to you in the bible there was man that was cripple had not walk in thirty eight years he had to hold on and wait for the troubling of the water for whoever step into the water would be healed then one day Jesus came and say would thou be healed the man reply was that someone always step in the water before me Jesus said take up your bed and walk and now the man is carrying what has been carrying him the man had to hold on his healing was coming to him sometimes it can get hard but hold on to God's love His will hold on to you will love the way His love make you feel oh what a feeling it is to be connected to His love in holding on hold on to faith have faith in God there was a centurion soldier that came to Jesus that his servant is at home sick he wanted Jesus to heal him Jesus was going to his home but he said I'm a man under authority when I tell one to come he cometh one to go he goeth he said if you will just speak the word my servant will be healed Jesus said that He have not found so greater faith in all Israel holding to faith in God in the storm if you get knock down hold on hold on to His love no matter what anyone says hold on you will get haters because when I was going through this you will have people want to see you down then up you can't let that stop you keep moving and hold on to God's love. Love is the most wonderful splendid thing love is caring and sharing the love that save me is a love like no other the love of God the love of my Father this love had my back this love is dependable. This love is everlasting this love is pure this love held on to me and I held on to it even when they wanted to control me I held on to the love of God Even I was feeling the vibes of the work of it I held on even through being laugh at I still held on this love never let me down I knew that I always could count on this love the love for him cause me to go into worship and praise no matter what I am determined to hold on in holding on to His love. There is no fear in His love. His love cast out all fear this love will shelter you in the storm this love has deliverance in it many of the affliction of the righteous but Lord deliver him out of them all his love will deliver on time He is never late always on time in holding on His love will never fail you when they try to press matter was days when I was press down but like the old songs say when nothing else will help love lifted me I held on to the love of God. Love is the high esteem that God has for His children and the high regard which they in turn should have for Him His love lifted me higher to a level that I didn't think I'll be when there is truly love Him you could do no one any evil because His love is in you that when His love is shown His love is all so an essential part of His nature He is love His Love is all so the personification of perfect love this love understand the power of this love will endure to the end so let us love God we love Him like He love us we will have no problem loving each other holding on to His Love.

CHAPTER EIGHT

His Love will Shine through the Darkness

Thou we may have dark day in the storm but His love will shine through the mist of it there is no darkness that's strong enough to prevent His love from shining through the bible shine darkness and the darkness comprehend it not no matter how dark that it may seem to that His love is able to shine in that the mist of the darkness in the dark days that I had when I went through His is my guiding light through the days of hurt and pain His love guide me through some dangerous things thing that was so dangerous that they counted me out but His love for me say not so this is my child my son He said in His word I will not fear what man can do unto me for the Lord is on my side His love is with me to guide me through those darkest days oh! How awesome His love is there two Greek words that means love:

(A) Phileo- means to have ardent affection and feeling a type of impulsive love.

(B) Agapo- means to have esteem or high regard.

Love is like oil to the wheels of obedience it enable us to run the way of God commandment this love never fails but flourishes the bible said that weeping may endure for a night but joy cometh in the morning many of times I would wonder how long is the night when is day coming but the love of God will shine through the darkest of your night His love shine when you can lay down and seethe night it be dark and when you began to start to see day breaking through you know that day is breaking through. It wants to be long it will be day full day light have broken through when there are dark days and there will be some but to know that God is light in Him there is no darkness at all even when you can't see your way out God always have a way out or a way of escape for you. He rule and He rang over the day and the night yes there was many dark days in my life but the shining of the love of God guided me through that trail that I went through one of the dark days was I told to drink ammonia and Pepsi soda I had to plead the blood of Jesus the situation that I been through with I've been surrounded with their work feeling attacked from all round me I could explain how are what those attacks felt like but to that love of God shinning in the mist of the darkness fasting and praying plays a big part in breaking the strong hold of the enemy there was a man that had a son that was a demon possess and the man took his son to the disciples but could not cast the spirit out and he took him to Jesus and He cast out he spirit and when they got alone with Jesus why couldn't they do that Jesus said this kind only come through but by fasting and praying there is a saying that says the dark is hour is just before the break of day and that hour can be extremely dark and tough but power of His love shine through that to deliver when it shows you the break of day it encourage to hold on a while longer when you make through it the bible says eyes have not seen ears have not heard neither have it enter in to the heart of man the good things God have in store for those that love Him in the bible there was a lady that was possess by an evil spirit and she brought her master great gain she would follow Paul and Aalas these men are servants of the most high God she did this continually until Paul turn in the name of Jesus Christ come out and she was delivered her dark ended of that right then the darkness of what I been through with the power of His love the light of His love shine and brought out that storm when God delivers you the enemy get mad angry at you that's what God delivered the woman and the one that had control of her could control her any more the light of God had shine upon her there also was a man that live in the graveyard crying and cutting himself with stones then they would bound him with chains and they have been pluck asunder by him and one day he came up Jesus and say what have we to do with the Jesus of Nazareth our time is not yet they knew who Jesus is Jesus said what is your name they said we are legion which means many this man had many demons in him Jesus told them to hush and to come out of the man the demons said where they wanted to go into the herd of swine feeding the Bible says that they ran to the water and they drown the darkness could out power of light the love of God will all ways shine through the light is what drew him out of darkness this love is the way the light and the light the journey through this was long and hard the love of this light brought me out and through some hard and to think that they thought that I was done and over with but God His love for me I can even tell when those demonic spirits was around I can smell them feel them work at me squeeze at me my feet they would feel like they was in a vice grip gripping my feet and my neck would be back they would actually speak from my neck and side say what they wanted to say they hiding working at me in the dark they would send spirit at even attack me in my sleep but the light of God have shine upon me to destroy the work of darkness I know that there is victory in Jesus there is power in the name of Jesus and there is wonder working power in the precious blood of the Lamb His blood is so powerful that one drop cause an earthquake the light is so powerful when it shine around Paul that it blinded him it knock off the beast he was on there is song that says walk in the light the beautiful light come where the dew drops where mercy shine bright shine all around me by day and by night Jesus the light of the world in the Bible the word said in ST. JOHN 11:1-44 Now a certain man was sick named Lazarus of Bethany the town of Mary and her sister Martha in verse 34

Jesus said where have you laid him they said unto him Lord come and see 35 Jesus wept Jesus wanted to know where Lazarus was where put him in verse 43 and 44 and when he thus had spoken he cried with loud voice Lazarus come forth and he that was dead came forth bound hand and foot with grave clothes and his face about with a napkin Jesus saith loose the him and let him go there is a song that says oh lamb of God I come just I am Lazarus came forth there was grave clothes on him but those clothes was taken off him when I was going through what I was going through with there was spirits trying to hold me back hindering spirits blockers haters witch and warlocks trying to hold me back but God loose me from there strong hold darkness don't like light the power of God light shine I'M 100% RELYING ON JESUS.

CHAPTER NINE

The Help of God's Love

I had to realize that I could fight this battle on my own I needed help in the bible in psalm 121 I will lift up my eyes unto the hills from whence cometh my help my help cometh from the Lord which made the heaven and earth He will not suffer thy foot to be moved he that keepeth thee will not slumber behold he that keepeth Israel shall neither slumber nor sleep the Lord is thy keeper the Lord is thy shade upon thy right hand. The sun shall not smite thee by day nor the moon by night. The lord shall preserve thee from all evil he shall preserve thy soul. The Lord shall preserve thy going out and thy coming in from this time forth and even for evermore through every battle every situation and with every enemy the Lord was David help when he had to face a lion and a bear the God of Israel was there for his help all that I been through God is there for my help He help me through one of the toughest storms that I ever been in I talk about it earlier in the book He help me in the book of psalms the Lord is on my side I will not fear what can man do unto me. He was right there for me through that. I've come to know for myself what a mighty God that I serve there are testimony from the bible but when you your own testimony when he showed up to help you when you for yourself see the mighty move of God take place before your very own eyes it like no other to see Him come to my aid there was one time I walk in the house there some stuff wipe on the wall or sprayed on there I could hardly breath I had to hurry and get out the door pray to shake it off He help me to breath I had silver dollar size sores on my legs making it hard for me to walk one my sister Linda put olive oil on my legs and she prayed and right before our eyes those silver dollars size sores shrank to dime size the Lord is my help he is a present help in the time of trouble you will have trouble but to that God is there to help you and to see you through it He help me make it through a painful storm nobody but God that was there for me when he all you got to depend on most of all He will help and want talk about you.

So many times I look up to the Lord for help the bible said when the enemy come in like flood He will lift up a slander many times I would hit in my back like if would have a bully on my back I would feel picking on my head the help of the Lord was right there with me one can put a thousand to flight two can put ten thousand to flight we can't make it by ourselves we need God's help God is not slack concerning his promise he love I'm with you even to the end of the world the bible said I can do all things through Christ Jesus that strengthen me it's His help that we got to depend on when the children of Israel was at the Red Sea the awesome power of God help them to cross the Red Sea they had the Red Sea in front of them they had a mountain on each side of them and Pharaoh army behind them they was trap no way out the enemy thought that he had them it's amazing when the enemy think that he got he thought that he had me for the Lord is my help thought he had me trap but God had always had a way of escape for me He brought out of that situation God help me through that storm in the bible Mu. 15:22-28 And behold a woman of Canaan came out of the same coast and cried unto him saying have mercy on me oh Lord thou son of David my daughter is vexed with a devil. But he answered her not a word and his disciples came and besought him saying send her away for she crieth after us.

But he answered and said I am not sent but unto the lost sheep of house Israel. Then came she and worship him saying Lord help me. But he answered and said it is not meet to take the children bread and to cast it to dogs and she said truth Lord yet dogs eat of the crumb's which fall from their master's table then Jesus answered and said unto her of women great is thy faith be it unto thee ven as thou wilt and her daughter was made whole from that very hour. The power of God's help faith Jesus acted on great was her faith the disciple wanted to send her away she not an Israelite none of that turn her away her main goal was that she wanted help she knew that Jesus is able to help her faith in God I love the saying of R W Sham bot you don't have no problem all you need is faith in God I had put full complete faith in God through the rain the strong winds I did not let that stop my faith in God it matter what looked like or what feel like I hold on to faith in God the bible declares and said the just shall walk by faith and not by sight we got to have faith in God faith please God.

The most amazing thing about God's help he's always there you may feel alone but you're not alone in the bible in the book of ST. MARK. 9: 17-29.

And one of the multitude answered and said Master I have brought unto thee my son which hath a dumb spirits and whosesoever he taketh Him he tearth him and he foamth from the mouth and gnaheth with his teeth and pineth away and I speak to thy disciples that they should cast him out and they could not. He answereth him and saith o faithless generation how long shall I be with you how long shall I suffer you bring him unto me. And they brought him unto him and when he saw him straightway the spirit is him and he fell on the ground and wallowed foaming. And he asked his father how long is it ago since this came unto him and he said of a child, and of times it hath cast him into the fire and into the waters to destroy him but if thou canst do anything have compassion on us and help us. Jesus said if thou canst believe all things are possible to him that believeth. And straight away the father of the child cried out and said with tears Lord I believe help thou my unbelief. When Jesus saw that the people came running together he rebuke the foul spirit saying unto him thou dumb and deaf spirit I charge thee come out of him and enter no more into him. And the spirit cried and rent him sore and came out of him and he was as one dead in so much that many said he is dead. But Jesus took him by the hand and lifted him up and he arose. And when he was come into the house his disciple asked him privately why could not we cast him out. And he said unto them this kind can come forth by nothing but by prayer and fasting the man needed help with a son that had a spirit that had him deaf and dumb the authority of Jesus He was moved with compassion in casting out the spirit that had the young man in this condition God freed the young man of what was controlling him I was in a condition not in the same way but in a sort of like manner a oppressing spirit was sent at me day in and day out a controlling spirit as well   at my mind my feet side I was always constantly under attack went to Jesus for help when I said I had to 100% depend on God I'm doing that right now for my every need I understand when David said I will lift up mine eyes unto the hills from whence cometh my help He is the greatest.

There is another scripture to look at Hebrew 4:16 Let us come boldly to the thorn of grace that we may obtain mercy and find grace to help in time of need he how we should come to the throne of grace how to come in Prayer that we may get mercy and grace.

CHAPTER TEN

Trusting in His Love

I once heard a story of a house wife with two kids her and her husband are born again believers it came up one Christmas and that there was no money in the house she was visit by an evangelist and the man of God knock on the door and she answered it he came in and say how are you she says fine he ask what was she doing I'm putting up this Christmas tree I'm trusting God come Christ enamoring there will be presents up under the trees he ask him to pray and he did and he left when Christmas came there was plenty of present up under the tree God truly bless them there an old song that said:

I will trust in the Lord until I die it's a continuing thing to do I remember saying God I will trust you no matter what I see or feel I trust you no matter what through the storm and through the rain I trust God through hard pain I trust God for my every need desires I place my trust in God a hurricane bring with it heavy rain flooding damaging winds destruction life storms bring with it pain destruction but through it all trusting God is the main key through it all you got to put your trust in Jesus he will make Everything alright. Trust means to put one's confidence in Psalms 33:21 For our heart shall rejoice in him because we have trusted in his Holy name having the confidence in his name is power in that name at that name every knee shall bow every tongue shall confess that Jesus Christ is Lord. That name Jesus carries authority in ST. JOHN 14:14 what so ever you ask in my name I will do it yes we got to trust God even when we can't see our way yet we got to trust in him the bible said there for I say unto you what things so ever ye desire. When ye pray believe that ye receive them and ye shall have them trusting God with our whole heart I remember years ago that a good friend was in the hospital he had a tumor on the brain they did surgery we went in to pray for him and while he was laying their unconscious his body started to jumping the power of God came in there so strongly that that his whole body was jumping and a week later his was home up walking around trust God my friends trust Him and wait on Him.

In trusting in God's love will get the menth that you need to make it on through to the other side I had to totally trust God in this God protect me in all of this from the work of my enemies their evil work was press around me and I trust God I stood on His word having the confidence in His name it power in His love and in His name that name carries power deliverance victory security you always can depend on that name authority is in that name to get to where God is I had to go through it but I never was alone while I went through I had to do is pray 2. faith 3. trust 4. read His word 5. stand on His word 6. praise those are things that did to make it out of that trust in sin His love His love never changes it is unchangeable.

This love is all powerful! It is unlimited He can do anything that is not inconsistent with His nature character His love possesses all-knowing and all knowledge His love is everywhere it is not confined to any part of the universe the name Jehovah/Yahweh in EX.3:4 gives full evidence that He is I AM that love is Jehovah Jireh the will provide that love is Jehovah Nissi the Lord is my banner in honor of Him He defeated thy enemies that love is Jehovah-shalom the Lord is peace that love is Jehovah-shammah the Lord is there even by trusting in His name brings you the victory when was in the storm I was in I will bless the

Lord at all time and His praise will continue be in my mouth praise Him any way no matter what and there are benefits for trusting in God the word benefit means good done or received a kindness or favor anything that is for the good of a person or thing in Psalms 68:19 Blessed be the Lord who daily loadeth us with benefits even the God of our salvation Selah there many different things with benefits jobs insurance but it's limited but God is loaded with it He will never run out PS.I 03:2 Bless the Lord oh my soul and forget not all His benefit we are not to forget about God's benefits how sweet it is to trust in Jesus. He got good benefits keep your trust in the Lord and guarantee you that everything will be alright there many things that we get from the benefits of trusting in God.

(A) JOY

PS.5:11 But let all those that put their trust in thee rejoice let them ever shout for joy because thou defendest them let them also that love thy name be joyful in thee. A benefit for trusting in God is joy the joy the world doesn't give and the world can't take it away the joy of the Lord is our strength.

(B) DELIVERANCE

PS.22:4.5 Our fathers trusted in thee they trusted and thou didst deliver them. They cried unto the and were delivered they trusted in thee and were not confounded deliverance is the next benefit we get from trusting God is a deliverer by trusting in Him He will bring you out Daniel the Hebrew boys Lazarus Peter mother in law just to name a few.

(C) Triumph

PS.0 My God I trust in thee let me not be ashamed let not mine enemies triumph over me. Yea let none that wait on that wait on thee be ashamed let them be ashamed which transgress without cause. Triumph from trusting God you get this triumph over your enemies.

(D) God's goodness

PS. 31:19 Oh great is thy goodness which thou hast laid up for them that fear thee which thou hast wrought for them that trust in thee before the sons of men. For trusting God, you will enjoy His goodness.

(E) MERCY

PS.32:10 Many sorrows shall be to the wicked but he that trusteth in the Lord mercy shall compass him about for trusting in the Lord you will get His mercy as the song says oh Lord have mercy.

(F) BLESSEDNESS

PS.40:4 Blessed is that man that maketh the Lord his trust and respecteth not the proud nor such as tum aside to lies. Blessed are you when you maketh the Lord your trust when we put our trust in Him blessing are on the way to you blessing are on the way for me with a reward from the Lord.

(G) SAFETY

PS 56:4,11 In God I will praise his word in God I have put my trust I will Not fear what flesh can do unto me. 11 In God I have put my trust I will not be afraid what can man do unto me safety is a benefit from trusting God will keep us safe from all harm and from the enemy and our enemies.

(H) GUIDANCE

PROV.3:5-6 Trust in the Lord with all thin heart and lean not unto Him own understanding. In all thy ways acknowlegd the Lord and He Will direct thy path a benefit of God guidance He will guide you into all truth where to go guide you even when you can't see your way.

Those are the benefit of trusting in God's love His benefits are much better last longer never changes stays the same he asks that we trust Him. Trusting in His love you have security.

CHAPTER ELEVEN

When God Fight the Battle You Gain the Victory

In the bible the word of God said when Joseph ate gotten word that they was going to be an act he call for a fast and as they stood the man of God stood in the midst of them and said fear not for the battle is not yours but the Lord's and he told them to stand still and see the salvation of the Lord when Josephate rose early in the morning that bowed his face to the ground and said believe in the Lord God and you will be establish believe His prophets so shall ye prosper God faught the battle but they got the victory they got silver and gold it took them three days to gather it all when God is fighting the battle it is good to be obedience to God in the battle do what ever He say to do when the Phillistines they had a champion by the name of Goliath. He would stand and challenge the Israelite talk about their God when David heard this he was angry who is this uncircumcised Philistine cursing the God of Israel David went to the brook and 5 smooth stones and went to face the giant the giant said what this a child I feed his flesh to the fowls of the air but David said you come to me with a sword and a spear but I in the name of the Lord God of Israel God guided the stone into the forehead of the Giant and he fell to the ground and David took the sword of the giant and cut his head off God fought the battle and David got the victory it was a long battle for me but God taught it I praise Him for it when Gedian one the judges of Israel when they had to fight they stood with thousands and Gedian ask that you that are afraid can leave and go home many of them left and went home God said that still to many they went to the river of water and God said them that lap water like a dog sat them to the side and He did they was do will to three hundred men and they went He had 100 men to stand there 100 hundred to stand here the other 100 men to stand and in front every man stood in his place each one had a pitcher in their hand they was to break the pitcher and shout and when they did it confuse them and they started killing each other God fought the battle.

It's a blessing when God gives you the victory over any situation no matter what it is there are people in battle with many different things many are battling drug addiction alcohol addiction sickness God will give you the victory and there are some that dealing with what I went with the battle is not mine it the Lord when David came home found their homes burned to the ground and David prayed and ask the Lord should I go up and the Lord said go and up to Zigglag he went the Lord fought the battle they recover their wives back you can be victorious in your battle God will fight your battle He is a God that never lost a battle when you check His track record.

So many victories and you will find out that He never lost a battle the battle that I was in which earth the attack of the enemy God taught it the battle was not mine it was the Lord the enemy already defeated foe the God of Abraham Isaac and Jacob not only He will fight for you He will hide you from your enemies when Saul was looking for David God cause a spider to weave a web to hide David and when Saul went in to the cave he could not find him in the time of trouble He shall hide me God will hide you from trouble you might be battling unforgiveness in the bible it said in Matt6:14- IS For if ye forgive men their trespasses your heavenly Father will also forgive you. But if ye forgive not men of their trespasses neither will your heavenly Father forgive you it's God's will for us to forgive when forgive it's to help you to gain the victory. The victory of Jesus Christ.

(A) Promised - Psalms 110:1-7

The Lord said unto my Lord sit thou at my right hand until I make thine enemies thy fool stool. The Lord shall send the rod of thy strength out of Zion rule thou in the midst of thine enemies. Thy people shall be willing in the day of thy power in the beauties of holiness from the womb of the morning thou hast the dew of thy youth. The Lord hath sworn and will not repent thou art a priest for ever after the order of Mel-chize-dek. The Lord at thy right hand shall through Kings in the day of his wrath. He shall judge among the heathen he shall fill the places with the dead bodies he shall wound the heads over many countries. He shall drink of the brook in the way therefore shall he lift up the head. This is the promise of Christ to make your enemies your foot stool that the victory another victory of Christ is

(B) His Resurrection, ACTS 2:29-36

Men and brethren let me freely speak unto you of the patriarch David that He is both dead and buried and his sepulcher is with us unto this day. Therefore, being a prophet and knowing that God had sworn with an oath to him that of the fruit of loins according to the flesh he would raise up Christ to sit on his thorn. He seeing this before spoke of the resurrection of left in hell neither his flesh did see corruption. This Jesus hath God raised up whereof we all are witness. Therefore, being by the right hand of God exalted and having received of the Father the promise of the Holy Ghost He hath shed forth this which ye now and hear.

For David is not ascended into heavens but he saith himself the Lord said unto my Lord sit thou on my right hand. Until I make thy foes thy footstool. Therefore, let all the house of Israel know assuredly that God hath made that same Jesus whom Ye have crucified both Lord and Christ. God promise to David that from his loins is going to be someone sit on his thorn and his world will never come to an end Christ got victory over death and the grave through His Resurrection He siueth on the right hand of the Father He came and died and rose from the dead to save all men kind with the shedding of blood there is no remission of sin.

(C) CHRIST RETURN REV.19: 11-21

And I saw heaven opened and behold a white horse and he that sat upon Him was called faithful and true and in righteousness he doth judge and make will. His eyes were as a flame of fire and on his head were many crowns and he had a name written that no man knew but he himself. And he was clothed with a vesture dipped in blood and his name is called the Word of God. And the armies which were in heaven followed him upon white horse clothed in fine linen white and clean. And out of his mouth goeth a sharp sword that with it he should smite the nation and rule them with a rod of iron and he treadeth the winepress of the fierceness and wrath of Almighty God. And he hath on his vesture and on his thigh a name written KING OF KING AND LORD OF LORDS. And I saw an angel standing in the sun and he cried with a loud voice saying to all the fowls that fly in the midst of heaven come and gather supper of the great God. That ye may eat the flesh of King and the flesh of captains and the flesh of mighty men and the flesh of horse and of them that sit on them and the flesh of all men both free and bond both small and great. And I saw the beast and the Kings of the earth and their armies gathered together to make war against him that sat on the horse and against his army. And the beast was taken and with him the false prophet that wrought miracles before him with which he deceived them that worshipped his image these both were cast alive into of fire burning with brimstone. And the remnant was slain with the sword of him that sat upon the horse which sword proceeded out of his mouth and all the fowls were filled with their flesh. The victory of Jesus Christ when comes to carry us home this story ends with a happy ending Jesus he is victorious.

VICTORY OF A CHRISTIAN

(A) THROUGH CHRIST PHIL.4:13

I can do all things through Christ which strengtheneth me. It through His strength we get the victory over whatever the situation is not our strength but His the Joy of the Lord is our strength you can do all through His power and it let us know that not some tings but all things barring our burdens.

(B) BY THE HOLY SPIRIT GAL.5: I 6, I 7.22, 25

This I say then walk in the spirit and ye shall not fulfil the lust of the flesh. For the flesh lusteth against the spirit and the spirit against flesh and these Are contrary the one to the others so that cannot do the things that ye would. By walking in the spirit of God we are in tune with God in fallowing the spirit and His guiding you will not do the things of the flesh Vs 22. But the fruit of the spirit is love joy peace long suffering gentleness goodness faith. Vs 25. If we live in the spirit let us also walk in the spirit. To walk in the spirit, you must live in the spirit to do that the spirit must be in you must have the Spirit of God the bible said if any man has not the spirit of Christ he is none of His.

WHAT THE CHRISTIAN HAVE VICTORY OVER

(A) FLESH Gal. 5: 16-21

This I say then walk in the spirit and ye shall not fulfil the lust of the flesh. For the flesh lusteth against the spirit and the spirit against the flesh and these are contrary the one to the other so that ye cannot do the things that you would. But if ye be led of the spirit ye are not under the law. Now the works of the flesh are manifest which the adultery formication uncleaned lasciviousness. Idolatry witchcraft hatted variance emulations wrath strife sedition heresies. Envying murders drunkenness reveling and such like of the which I tell you before I have told you in time past that they which do such things shall not inherit the kingdom of God. When you accept Jesus as Lord and savior He give victory over the flesh there was old commercial that says starve a cold and feed a fever but if you starve the flesh and feed the spirit you will not walk in the flesh.

(B) John 5:4

For whatsoever is born of God overcometh is born of God overcometh the world and this is the victory that overcometh the world even our faith. By being born of God makes you an overcomer we overcame because of what Christ did by going to Calvary overcome the world by believing that Jesus is the Son of God.

(C) James 4:7

Submit yourselves therefore to God resist the devil and he will flee from you. Submit, accept or yield to a superior force or to the authority or will of another person when we submit to God to his will only then we can resist the devil and he will flee the enemy don't mind letting you know that he means business we have to do the same let him know that we mean business lamefully sublimed to you Lord.

CHAPTER TWELVE

Bouncing Back

Sometimes life can through a hard blow that can knock us down but the blessing thing is that we don't have to stay down we can get up from it a quitter never win and a winner never give up when a fighter gets knock down even if he have to crawl to the ropes to pull himself up to get back into the fight he is letting his opponent know I'm back in the fight don't count me out when the deliver you a hard blow he thinks it's over with but it's not over till God said it's over he lets him know that he is bouncing back the most greatest bounce back is that of our Lord Jesus Christ when He waited on and whip all through the night spit on slap in the face led from judgment hall to judgment hall to have the same peoples say crucify Him went on a hill call Calvary nail to a cross and hang out there from the sixth to the ninth hour then they laid him in a barrowed tomb they thought He was counted out it was over with He was in there for three days and three nights He bounce back from all what was done to Him early that morning He got up with all power in His hands death where is your sting grave where is your victory Jesus is victorious they gave money to spread the lie that Jesus disciples stole the body but truth always prevail. He appeared to His disciples the two on the enmuss road and then to 500 at one times there's proof that He rose He is alive and well there is a song that said an empty tomb prove that my savior lives most He lives in me I remember some years ago that my father was in an accident his leg was broken he was in the hospital he had to be off work for a while he is the provider for the family my father is a pastor and a praying man he bounce back from that accident his leg was got healed through that whole time the Lord provided For us yes while you ae bouncing back God will provide for everything that you need to make it I never seen the righteous forsaken nor His seed begging bread I owe it to Jesus my blessing Savior through Him I bounce back from pain hurt which erased and being attack by the enemy.

There are a few that I would like to talk about that went through some tough situation and they bounce back God bless them to do so things that Would cause some folks to throw in the towel but it's the trust that they have in the God that they serve by trusting Him I don't know what you had to bounce back from home for closure car repossessed house robbed house fire many are bouncing back from tornados hurricanes sickness in the bible there was ten men that were lepers and when you have leprosy you was considered unclean and you would living on the outside of town you could Not come into the city for nothing but one day Jesus came through the ten of them carne to Him and He healed all ten of them Retold them to go show yourself to the priest and the priest would have to say that they are clean And when they was pronounce clean only one of them carne to tell Jesus Thank you and Jesus wasn't there ten cleansed where are the nine this man Bounce back from being a leper to being healed by Jesus and carne to tell Him thank you in everything give thanks when the Lord bless us we got to tell Him thank you to get to some period that bounce back.

(A) Isaac Gen 26: 12-28

Then Isaac sow in that land and received in the same year and hundredfold and the Lord blessed him. Isaac grew great he had possession of flocks herds the Philistines envied him they told him that he had to leave and when He left he notice that the Philistines had block up the wells that his Father Abraham had dug so he to redig the wells that his Father had dug he had fresh water to drink Isaac bounce back from what the Philistine. Did they Wanted him to thirst to death but God bless him to prosper many times there are peoples will do anything to you because they don't want to see you prosper it's ok when they do but when God began to bless you it's a whole another thing I had to bounce back from some things that I will talk about later in this chapter but there one instance that happen where that I had my bike stolen I bounce back not long after that I got my first car from peddling to driving.

(B) Joseph Gen. Chapter 37

In the story you will find that Jacob love Joseph more than his brethen. He gotten him in his old age and Jacob gave him a coat of many colors his brothers they hated him when you have a love for God he blesses you. You will have haters to you will even have haters that will hate you without a cause a portion of what I went through with was because of being hated and among other thing jealousy etc. Joseph had a dream he told to his brothers they hated him even the more. Sometimes God will use your haters to push you into your destiny now Jacob sent Joseph to scheme to check on his brothers and when they've seen him coming they said here comes this dreamer they took hold of Joseph and place him in a hole and took his coat of many colors and kill one of the animals and they said among them sells we will tell their father that a wild animal killed him they dipped Joseph's coat in the blood of the calf about that time came a man from Egypt they sold Joseph and did what they planned they told Jacob that Joseph is dead they showed him his coat that their father gave him they told him that a wild animal killed him this hated Jacob they cared nothing about what this would do to their father the man from Egypt took Joseph to his house left his in charge Joseph brothers meant it for evil but is going to turn it for his good while the master was away his wife tried to get Joseph to lay with her but he refuse to do so she grab his coat he came out of it and ran away for his life when her husband came home she lied and said that he force himself on her the maser got mad and had Joseph put in prison for a space of time and there was two men in the cell with him and the baker and the butler they both had dreams and Joseph interpreted them both the butler was restored back to his Job but the baker was hang when the butler got out he forgotten all about Joseph until Pharaoh had a dream and then the butler remember Joseph he told pharaoh about Joseph the King had him brought in and Joseph told pharaoh what his dream meant pharaoh gave him a ring made him over the food he bounce back from all he been through and falsely accused in a pit put in prison and now in a place God worked all out for his good.

There are many more that bounce back John was put on the Isle of Patmos Rev 1:9 Paul beaten and left for dead ship wreck 2Con 11:25 the Hebrew Boys Dan the 3rd chapter in the burning fiery furnace Daniel in the lion den Dan.6 the chapter. Job lost everything he had he bounce back and God Bless him double the whole book I bounce back from all that I been through I've been low to go high to go over and not under I went through being opressed by the enemy and the which erath but I bounce back from it all.

CHAPTER THIRTEEN

Love Bringing You Out Unharm

God will bring you out with no hurt completely unharmed the meaning of the word is (not having sustained physical moral or mental injury) as I went through God brought me out unharmed when His hand of protection is on you the devil can do you no harm in the bible in Is 43:1-2 The Lord that created thee Jacob and He that formed the fear not for I have called by thy name thou art mine. When passed through the waters I will be there with thee and through the rivers they shall not over flow thee when walketh through the fire thou shall not be burned neither shall the flame kindle upon thee. You see whatever your river may be we serve a God that will bring you out unharmed I was attacked in the back many of times but God was right there to deliver me I remember when I was a little boy me and some friends was running and playing and I trip and fell and there was this stick that suck up out of the ground when I feel my head was turn just right if God had not had my turn just right the stick would have stook me through my right eye through the brain God brought me through unharmed in Daniel the third chapter Nebuchadnezzar the King made an image of gold whose height was three score cubits and the breath thereof was six cubits he set it up in the plain of Dura in the province of Babylon. Then Nebuchadnezzar the King sent to gather the prince the governors and the captains the judge. The treasurers the counselors the sheriffs and all the rulers of the and all the rulers of the province to come to the dedication of the image that Nebuchadnezzar the King had set up verse 5 that at what time ye hear the sound of cornet flute harp sackbut psaltery dulcimer and all kind of music ye fall down and worship the image the golden image that the King hath set up if you falleth not down and worship the image you will be cast into a burning fiery furnace. There are certain Jews that whom thou hast set over the affairs of the province of Babylon Shadrach Meshach and Abed-nego these have not regarded thee they serve not thy God nor worship the golden image which thou heat up this anger the King he demand that the Hebrew boys be brought to him now they let the King know that they want going to bow nor worship the image the King Wain rage he commanded that he furnace be heated seven times hotter now he had mighty men to bind the three Hebrew boys to put them in the furnace the heat from this furnace was so hot that it killed the mighty men that put the Hebrew boys in the furnace I notice something here that God was with the Hebrew boys before they was put in the furnace they would had died with the might y men that put them in why didn't they die in the fire they stood up for God now God is standing up for them He backing up what the Hebrew boys told the king the God that we serve will deliver us out of your hands o king when he arose he looked in the furnace didn't we put three men in the furnace they answer him yes behold in see four his eyes were that he may see the son of God he saw the great I am the lily of the valley the bright and morning star he asks them who is this God that will deliver you out of mine hands he saw the God that he ask them about they was loose walking in the furnace he ask them to come out of the furnace they came out of the furnace and when they came out the fire had no power over them their hair was not singed their coat was not burn up the fire did them no harm they came out unharmed when I went through the heat of the witch craft that I went through with it was very tense but God brought me out unharmed the bible said many are the affliction of the righteous but the Lord deliver him out of them all there is power in the blood of the lamb it's a blessing when you are going through and God is with you every step of the way even in the midst of being lied on and false accused and being attack by the spirit of confusion God is with me it don't matter what it look like to know that God is with me even through mean thing being said and have been said about me to that I serve a God that blessing to rise above it all through the storm and rain God bless me to make it the weapons of our warfare are not cornal but they are mighty through God to the pulling down of strong hold and most of all stand strong in the LORD in the power of His might the next person that came out unharmed is Daniel. Daniel the 6th chapter it pleaded Darious to set over the kingdom and hundred and twenty princes which should be be over the whole kingdom. And over these three president of whom Daniel was first that the princes might give accounts unto them and the king should have no damage. Then this Daniel was preferred above the president and princes because an excellent spirit was in him and the king thought to set him over the king thought to set him over the whole realm. Then the president and princes sought to find occasion against Daniel concerning the kindom but they could find none occasion nor fault for such as he was faithful neither was there any error or fault found in him. So the princeses and the presidents got together to plan against Daniel they establish royal statute and to make a firm decree that whosoever shall ask a petition of any God or man for thirty days save of thee o king he shall be cast into the den of lions they ask the king to sign the writing when Daniel knew that the writting was sign he went into his house his window open toward Jerusalem he prayed three times a day making supplication to befor his God know they go to tell the king that Daniel wapraying to His God so the had to go through with the decree that he has sign they put Daniel in the lions den but the king said to Daniel the God that you serve He will deliver you the king went to his chambers fasting and praying all night the king rose early in the morning went in a bury to the den of lions when he got there he cried out Daniel servant of the living God Daniel answerd and said my God have sent his angel and have shut the lions mouth. They have not hurt me the king was happy he had Daniel taken up out of the den he had those men who accused Daniel and they cat them in the den of lions them their wives and their childrens the lions destroyed them all breaking their bones the mighty delivering power of God brought Daniel out unharmed in the twelve chapter of acts Peter was put in prison with four quotations of soldiers to keep him but there was a prayer meeting was going on in his behalf God sent an Angel to smote Peter on the side and said arise and follow me and when he got up his chain fell off Peter thought that he seen a vision then he came to know that it ws the Lord he came out of prison unharmed God was right there to deliver him it's a blessing to have people praying for you sincere prayer be going on for you.

CHAPTER FOURTEEN

Love Breaking the Chains of the Strong Hold

The love of God is so incredibly wonderful and so powerful chains keep you bound as the songs said there is power in the name of Jesus to break every chain no matter what chain that may have you bound the love of God is able to break that chain may holding you chains have names there is a controlling chain use to control you in the bible there was a woman that brought her masters much gain they had the chain of control on her she follow Paul and Salius chatting servants off the most high God Paul stop and turn a cast that spirit out of her the chain of control was broken she was free God freed her of that spirit of control brought her out of it and when God do something like that it makes your enemies made it cause them to do something even more drastic then before the reason I know because I have been through it one thing after another one of the thing I know that I was coming out victorious that God will break every stronghold of mine enemies and to deliver me out of the hands of mine enemies chain was use a fetters where with prisoners were bound (Jude 16:21 2 Sam 3:34 2 kings 25:7 Jer 39:7 sometimes for the sake of greater security the prisoner was attached by two chains to two soldiers as in the case of Peter Acts 12:6 when the angel touch Peter and those chain feel off of him there are many kinds of chains that holding many people but I'm here to let you know that the awesome love of God power is able to break and destroy those chains the chain that held me wathe working of which erath the power of God love broke that chain that I'm no longer bound and also the chain of the python spirit this spirit comes to squeeze the life out of you but the power of God love broke that chain in the bible in Isaiah Chapter 6:1-8 In the day that Uzziah died I saw also the Lord sitting upon a throne high and lifted up and His train filled the temple. Above it stood the seraphim each had six wings with twain he saw he covered his feet and with twain he did fly.

And one cried unto another and said Holy is the Lord of host the whole earth is full of his glory. And the post of the door moved at the voice of him that cried and the house was filled with smoke. Then said I woe is me for I am undone because Iam a man of unclean lips and I dwell in the mist of a people ofunclean lips for for mine eyes have seen theking the Lord of host. Then flew one of the sersphims unto me having a live coal in his hand which he had taken with the tongs from off the altar and he laid it upon m y mouth and said lo this hath touch thy lips and thine iniquity is taken away and thy sin purged. Also I heard the voice of the Lord saying whom shall I send and who will go for us? Then said here am I send me his chains was uncleaness but the love of touch his lips clean them and removed his iniquity if your chain is uncleanness the power of God's love can break that chain and clean you from all unrighteous. There was a woman that had the issue of blood for 12 years been to the doctor the matter got worse when she heard that Jesus was passing through she touched the hem of His garment and when she did she was healed instantly her chain was sickness the power of God love broke that chain of sickness her body was healed as we said there many differnt kinds of chains that holding people bound in. In St. JOHN 5:1-9 After this there was a feast of the Jews and Jesus went up to Jerusalem. Now there is at Jerusalem by the sheep market a pool which is called in the Hebrew tongue Bethesda having five porches. In these lay a great multitude of impotent folk of blind halt withered waiting for the moving of the water. For an Angel went down at a certain season into the pool and trouble the water whosoever then first after the troubling of the water stepped in was made whole of whatsoever disease he had. And a certain man was there which had infirmity thirty and eight years. When Jesus saw him lie and knew that he had been now a long time in that care he saith unto him will thou be made whole? The impotent man answered Him. Sir I have no man when the water is trouble to put me into the pool but while I am coming another steppeth down before me. Jesus saith unto him rise take up thy bed and walk. And immediately the man was made whole and took up his bed and walked and on the same day was the sabbath. Now this man chain was an infirmity that he was was unable to walk the power of love walk up to him and ask him will thou be made whole the man was healed immediately that chain of infirmity was broken.

THE DIFFFRENT CHAINS THE POWER OF GOD'S LOVE IS ABLE TO BREAK

Let me say there is no chain that he could not break.

(A) Lying - the bible said a liar would not tarry in his eye sight all liars shall have their part in the lake. He is able to break that chain of lying if the enemy have connected to the chain of lying his love is able to break that chain and free you. In the bible in Acts 5:1-10 But a certain man name Ananias as with Sapphira his with sold possession. And kept back part of the price his wife also being privy to it and broughta certain part and laid it at the apostle feet. But Peter said Ananias why hath satan filled thin heart tolie to the Holy Ghost and to keep back part of the price of the land. While it was not thine own and after it was sold was it not thin own power why hast thou conceived this thing in thin heart thou hast not lied unto me but unto God Ananias hearing these words fell down and gave up the ghost and great fear came on all them that heard these things. As you read on the same happened to his wife.

(B) Envying - Feeling uneasiness at the superior condition and happiness another or mortification experienced at the supposed prosperity and happiness of another in the bible there was a man by the name king Ahab and another man by the name of Naboth and he had a vineyard that he was going to pass down to his sons this vineyard has always been in the family when Naboth told him no he felt displeased about it he went home and Jezebel ask him what the matter he told her that Naboth would not sale him his vineyard and Jezebel forged the king signature and had Naboth and his sons killed so Ahab can have the vineyard the power of God's love can break this chain.

(C) Betray - To violate confindence by diclosing a secrete or that which was entrusted to expose followed by the person or the thing as my friend betrayed me or betrayed the secret Judas betrayed Jesus.

(D) Backbitting - The act of slandering the absent calumny.

(E) Adultery - The violation of the marriage bed a crime or an injury wnich introduces or may introduce into a family a spurious offspring God said the adulter He will judged.

(F) Jealousy - Suspicious apprehensive of rivalship uneasy through fear that another has withdrawn or may withdraw from one the affection of a person he loves or enjoy some good which he desires to obtain followed by of and applied both to the object of love and to the rival. When Saul eyed David the womans was singing Saul killed his thousand David killled his ten thousand Saul throwed a javelin at David trying to kill him.

(G) Homosexaulty - Is abomination hence defilement pollution in physical sense or evil doctrines and practices which are moral defilement idols and idolatry are called abominations. God said one man and one woman He made male and female there is no man born with a female in him it is a life style that the person took on we serve a God that merciful and full of love He is able to break that chain.

In the bible in the book of Galations Chapter 5: 19-21 Now the works of the flesh are manifest which are these adultery fimication uncleanness lasciviousness. Idolatry witchcraft hatred variance emulations wrath strife seditions heresies. Envvying murders drunkenness revellings and such like of the which I tell you before as I have also told you in time past that they which do such things shall not inherit the kingdom of God.

CHAPTER FIFTEEN

I'm Glad that Love Came

In the word of God, it said For God so love the world that He gave His only begotten Son that whosoever believe in Him shall not perish but have eternal life. Love was right there when the Father say let us make man love began the createth work of God in St. John Chapter one it said in the beginning was the word and the word was with God and the word was God love reach down into the dust of the ground and made man love promise Abraham that his descendants would be like the sand on the sea shore love is not slack concerning his premises love spoke to Moses from a burning bush to go to Egypt to tell pharaoh to let my people go love wrestle with Jacob to the break of day Jacob said I let go until you bless me his name was change from Jacob to Isreal love came down through 42 generation when love was born in place Bethlehem the wise men seen His stare in the east.

King Harod wanted to when the star appear he had his men to search the the scripture and he found out about the birth of love he told the wise men to go and worship love and when you have found Him bring me word that I may go and worship Him when they found love laying in a manger in swaddling clothes they brougt love Frankincense and myrrh gold but God warn the wise men in a dream not to go to Hadrod but go go home in a nother direction they did as God said when Hadrod saw that he wamark he Had male boys killed from 2 years old down trying to kill love but God showed Joseph in a dream to leave Hadrod seek love to kill Him so Joseph went to Egypt so the prophecy can be fulfilled I have call my son out of Egypt when love grow up he fasted 40 days and 40 nigthts when came off the fast He hunger then the devil came unto if you be the Son of God command these stones to be made bread love said man shall not live by bread alone but by every word that procedeth out of the mouth of God.

After the confrontation the devil left for a season then love came down to the Jordan river to be baptise now John was preaching in at the river saying repent for the kingdom of God is at hand but there is one who is mighter thine I who I'm not worthy to stoop down to unloosen he is pefferred before me and when John seen Jesus he said behold the Lamb of God I should be baptize by you Jesus suffer it to be so to fufill all righteousness and when John baptize Jesus when love came up out of the water the heaven open unto love and he saw the spirit of God descending like a dove and lighting on him him and low voice from heaven saying this is my beloved Son in whom I am well pleased.

When love came off the fast He began His public ministry preach on repent for the kingdom of God is at hand love went by the sea of Galilee and saw two brothers Simon and Andrew love aaid unto them follow me and I will make you fisher of men then it grew from two to twelve love went to a wedding and He turn water into wine this is the limp miracle that love did love is still in the miracle working business there was a man of the Pharisee named Nicodemus that came to love at night love talk to him about being bom again love met a woman at a well when love told her about what she doing and that the water that he will give her she will never thirst again she drop her water pots and went and told them come see a man that told me all that I did love went up to Jerusalem there was a pool call Bethesda having five porches. There was a man sick for thirty-eight years love walk up to him and say will thou be made whole and love reach out and caught by the hand and he was healed immediately love took two fish and five loafs of bread and feed five thousand men not counting the woman and the childrens the Disciples were way out in the ocean it was dark love came unto them walking on the water they thought it was a spirit but love said it is I be not afried but Peter said love if it is you bid meto come love said come Peter step out of the boat and walked on water but Peter look at the waves the wind and started to sink Peter said love save me love reach out and saved him the same love is reaching out to lost right now who so ever will let him come all that come unto love he will in no wise cast out love pass by and saw a man blind from his birth love spit on the ground and made clay of the spit anointed the eyes and told him 10 go wash in the pool of Silom the obeyed and came seeing. There was a certain man sick by the name of Lazarus.

Mary and Martha sent for love to come love stayed two more days where he was. After that Lazarus died now when love was on his way there Mary met him and said love if you had been here my brother would not have died and as he went a little farther Martha came unto and said the same thing but love looked at her and said I am the resurrection and the life those but yet shall he live and he said show me where you have laid him the short is verse in the bible love wept love went to the tomb were Lazarus was love said Father thank you for you have heard me but for the benefit of those standing around may believe love said take away the stone love cried out with a loud voice and said Lazarus come forth the dead got up came forth with grave clothes love said loose the man and let him go before this Lazarus had been dead four days and they said by this time he stinketh.

But I am reminded that there is a song that said Oh Lamb of God I come just as Jam Love want you to come to him just as you are stinking with the sins of the world love want you to come unto him the smell of cigarettes adultery whoremonger fornicator addicted to porn alcohol drugs or your grave clothes stealing lying wrath jealousy cheating gambling hypocrite no matter what it is love will deliver you. Now it's time for the pass over as love sat with them at supper satan put in the heart of Judas to betray love love got up push his garment to the side to wash the disciples feet and when that was finish they went to the garden and love said wait while I go under and pray love went and prayed not my will but your will be done love came and found them sleeping and said can't you watch with me one hour love said watch and pray that you enter not into temptation then Judas came with the council then Judas said to him who I kiss at him when one of the soldiers reach at love peter took his sword and cut off the mans ear love said put up your sword those who live by the sword shall perish by the sword they took love from judgment hall to judgment hall the paid false accuser to lie on love love came before pilot pilot wife said have nothing to do with this man he trouble me pilot said bring me some water to wash my hands I want no part of crucifying an innocent man the same one that said Hosana blessed is He that comes in the name of the Lord now they cry free Barbarous and put love on the eros. They beat love with 32 strips put thorns on love head they took love to a place call scull love went through the main streets of Jerusalem they put love on the cross love hang from the 9th to the 6th hour love said it is finish love gave up the ghost drop his head in the lock of his shoulders they put love in a borrowed tomb love was in there for three days and nights but early that Sunday morning love got up walk out of the tomb love has risen with all power in his hands this love that went through for us I'm so glad that he did through his jam able to do what Paul said to the Philippians 3:13-14 Brethen! count not myself 10 have apprehended but this one thing! Do forgetting those things which are behind me and reaching forth unto those things which are before. I press toward the mark forthe prize of the high calling of God in Christ Jesus through his I forgave and let it go.

CHAPTER SIXTEEN

The Power of Love

IN PRAYER

The bible says men ought to always pray and not faint spending time in prayer is so important let's look at something that concerning with prayer

Communication - Is with God because He is personal.
Faith - The most meaningful prayer comes from a heart that places its trust in the God who has acted in the spoken in the Jesus of history and the teaching of the bible.

Worship - In worship we recognize what is of highest worth — not ourselves others or work but God. Only the highest divine being deserves our highest respect.

Confession - Awareness of God's holiness leads to consciousness of our own sinfulness.

Adoration - God is love and he has demonstrated His love in the gift of His Son.

Praise - The natural outgrowth of faith worship confession and adoration is praise.

Thanksgiving - All was unthankful because we think we have not received what we deserve but if we got what we deserve God has been at work on our behalf in countless ways so in everything give thank even for discipline that is unpleasant.

Dedicated - Christ example does not require us to withdraw from society but to render service to the needy in a spirit prayer He wept over Jerusalem in compassionate prayer.

Request - Prayer is not only response to God's grace as brought to us in the life and work of Jesus and the teaching of scripture prayer is a request to a personal Lord who answer as He knows best.

Effectiveness - Prayer has power over everything God can intelligently act in any part of the universe or human history.

In the bible prayer constantly went on for Peter bound but prayer was lost Peter didn't worry about nothing he was 100% trusting God he went to sleep not worrying what was going to happen the next day didn't fear about it His life is hide in Christ he is resting peacefully he that dweleth in the secret place of the most shall abide under the shadow of the all mighty the angel came awaking him arise get up and get dress and fallow me his chain fell off you never know who is praying for you peter had 16 guards around Him God kows just how to deliver you out of the hand of your enemies God don't want you to worry about nothing God brought Peter out of a natural prison but there are many in a spiritual prison behind the bars of being mistreated hurt rejected abused molested lying all manner of evil about you depression being oppress of the devil prayer will bring you out of that prison.

CHAPTER SEVENTEEN

The Sun Will Shine Again

Sun a star that sustains life on the earth being the source of heat and light usually the word sun as used in the bible refers to the heavenly body that rises in the morning shines through the day and sets in the evening PS. 84: II God is called a sun and shield meaning He send light and heat and also gives protection God created the sun therefore it was not worthy of worship by people. The song or saying behind every dark cloud is sunshine I went through of dark days wondering when was the sun going to shine again PS.30:5 weeping may endure for a night but joy cometh in the morning. The cloud was symbolic of God presence the pillar of cloud leading the Israelite in the wilderness. The sun is a powerful light to rule the day this great light that rule the day plant life depends on this light there some that need the direct sun light those are the plant that goes through the heat of the sun I think about the person that goes through the heat of a trail the love of the Lord help them to make it through that even in the midst of it all you can still have joy it may not feel good going throgh it the flesh may feel the vibes of that thing but it's who you have on the in side Jesus Christ prayer plays a very important key to it all Paul said in the book of Phillipians I can do all things through Christ that strengthen me in Gal 2: 20 I am crucified with Christ nevertheless I live yet not I but Christ liveth in me and the life which I now live in the flesh I live by the faith of the Son of God who loved me and gave him self for me now there plants that you can't put in the sun light because it can not take it when you are going through it don't give up on God hold on to God unchanging hand He is a God that will not Leave you nor forsake you when I look at flowers I see the sun shine on them in a nursery class I Iearn that when the sun shine on a plant in the stem of that plant it makes a solution called simple sugar to send out to the whole plant when it start the close of the day and the sun is going down and the night shade appear that plant don't seem to worry because it knows that the sun is going to shine again it goes throgh the night loooking for the shining of the sun as it goes through the night waiting for the sun to appear when the break of day it seems like the plant stand tall it seees the sun is rising if that plant could speak it would say here comes the sun the plant seems to lift its leaves you know when we are going through a trail God still want us to give Him praise the psalm is said from the rising of the sun the going down the same God name is to be praise. In Mau 5:45 That ye maybe the children of your Father which is in heaven for He maketh His sun to rise on the evil and on the good and sendeth rain on the just and on the unjust I want to talk about another Son this Son is the Son of God a Son that they thought that was not going to shine any more this Son fame Has went out about this Son people was coming from all around to see this Son to be healed people was made to kill this Son but He escape though the crowd this Son said in the Gospel of John the 14th chapter whatsoever you ask in my name I will do it this Son ask the disciples who do men say that I am some say you are John the Baptist others say you are Elijah but who do ye say that I am Peter said that thou art the Christ the Son of the Living God   the Son said to Peter flesh and blood have not revel that nuto you but of my Father which is in Heaven this Son have 7 I AM in the book of ST. JOHN I AM- THE BREAD OF LIFE. THE LIGHT OF THE WORLD.THE GATE.THE GOOD SHEPHERD. THE RESURRECTION AND THE

LIFE. THE WAY THE TRUTH AND THE LIFE. THE TRUE VINE. This Son was asleep on a boat they waup on the u per deck a storm came up the wind and the waves carne up on the ship the disciples was afraid they woke up the Son of God saying Lord do you care that we Parish the Son says oh ye of little faith He got up and rebuke the wind and the waves and there was a great calm the disciples said among themselves what manner of man is that even the wind and the water obey Him   this son says no man cometh unto the Father but by me the blood of this Son is able to clean you from your sins this Son hung bleed and died for the sins of the world when they crucified this Son they thought in their mind that they had stop this Son for shining this Son when He died the sun stop shining it got dark the bible says that the old patriarch got up out of their grave and walked the streets of Jerusalem this Son was pirce in His side down came blood and water this Son went down in the grave and had a revival meeting got the keys this SAID DEATH WHERE IS YOUR STING AND GRAVE WHERE IS YOUR VICTORY. This Son walked out of that grave with all power in His hand the sun go down in the east and it rises in the west to shine the next following day but this Son early that morning rose from the dead to shine for ever more to give light to a dark world this Son Peter says I'm not worthy to be crucified like Him they turn him up side down. They thought that this Son was not going to shine again but what they did not know Sunday was coming the Son got up and one day this day is coming soon that the sun will be done away with the Son will be all the light that we need this Son is the light of the world.

CHAPTER EIGHTEEN

Waitlng on Love To Show Up

Love knows how to show up and when to show up when the Hebrew boys was in the fire furnace love shadowed up Daniel in the lion den love showed up on time when David face Goliath love showed up in Isiah the bible says they that wait on the Lord shall renew their strength they shall mount up with wing. They run and not be weary walk and not faint in the book of psalm it says wait on the Lord and He shall strengthen thin heart Lazarus waited in the grave for four days then he was resurrected. Waiting to be inactive until someone or something happens sometimes it can be hard to do impaction to wait for God to bless wait is to remain in readiness or expectation in scripture the word waits normally suggest the anxious yet confident expectation by God's people that the Lord will intervene is the working on your behalf waiting out of hope here are some scripture on waiting on the Lord before I do that let's take a brief moment what to do while waiting.

(1) keep trusting
(2) keep praying
(3) keep beleiving
(4) keep reading God's word
(5) stay encourage
(6) keep the faith

(7) stay in service
(8) keep worshipping the Lord

Scripture on waiting

with the souI-------ps 62:1;5 with quietness-----lam 3:25-26 with patience-----ps40:1

with courage---- 27:14

all the day---- ps 25:5

Continually----Hos12:6

With great hope -- ps 130: 5-6 with crying --- ps: 69:3

As you read be blesin reading them as I did I stood on His word everything is going down but the word of God.

CHAPTER NINETEEN

Keeping the Faith in Love

Faith is a belief in or confident attitude toward God involving commitment to His will for one's life according to Hebrews 2 faith was already present in the experience of many people in the old testament as key element of their spiritual lives.

I had to have faith and hold on to it keeping it in God and God alone. He knows and and saw what I was going through but He let me know I got you in my Hands is upon you I know that He will see me through it all as the song says I'm in His care His loving arms around me so no evil can not harm me. The Bible said cast all your cares on Him for He cares for your that is put all worries your concerns on Him He's the one that is able to fix it Eph.3:20 now unto Him that is able to do exceeding abundantly above all that we are think He is a God that can do anything but fail.

I have faith in this love andso did the one's in the old testament.

Abel faith please God Abel a shepherd brought his offering to God the firstling of the sheep's the best God accepted Abel offerring in the new Testament Abel offered a more excellent sacrifice then Cain also Abel righteous giving God the best of offering praise and worship Abel had faith in God you got faith in God and in God's favor not every is going to be happy for you not even family as you can see Cain saw God accepted Abel offering jealousy arise in Cain that he killed his brother Abel did and gave God what wanted the best of his live stock. Cain could have gotten it right with with God by the conversation God had with him many is going to mist out on going back with Jesus because refusing to get right with God gives the Lord their lives now is the acceptable time as old song said get right with God and do it now. Enoch - in his case the staunent was not made (then he died) as it was with the other males he walks with God walk is the biblical expression for fellowship and obedience that results in divine favor his walk lasted 300 years and God took him away he had one testimony that he please God he walks with God by faith I walk with in God and still walking in faith in God in obedience to Him and fellowship faith.

In His word keep walking through the storm keep walking with your head held high God said that he will your head lifted above your enemies no matter what I think that I was still able to walk in faith with my head held up above my enemies it was through His love I was able to do it.

Noah the son of Lameach and the Father of Shern Ham and Japeth a hero of faith building the ark God's instrument in saving mankind from total destruction by the flood.

Noah lived at a time when the whole earth was filled with violence and corruption yet Noah did not allow the evil standard of his day to rob him of fellowship with God I did the same I would let my faith get rob from me so my brother and sister keep the Faith in God I some times it could looked very tough in the storm but the love of God will bless you to sail through the storm some times you might get turn down but your turn down is not a let down what you need God got it.

So Noah obeyed God he stood as the only one who walked with God he was righteous man God single out Noah there may come a time that God will sing you out if He choose to get a certain job done. He chose Noah to build the ark God is going to send a flood Noah and his family survived that is the main thing l said to myself I will survive out of all that been through

I survived in the mist of the storm that I went through one of the scripture that I kept with me the just shall walk by Faith and not by sight.

Abraham - (Father of a multitude) The primary model of faithfulness for Christian while living in Huran at the age 75 Abraham received a call from God to go to a land unknown the land of promise Abraham that he would make him and his descendants a great nation his wife Sarah was childless Abraham obeyed God with no hint of doubt or disbelief he took his wife and his nephew lot and went to the land that God would show him   a man of faith obeying God steping out on faith that what I did reading this as I was writting this book sitting in my sister den God spoke to me where He wanted me to go so I began to make preparation to go where He wanted to go have faith in God He's still working miracles though things seemed quite difficult but Abraham faith in God promises allowed him to trust in the Lord.

Moses - The Hebrew Prophet who delivered the lsrealites from Egyptian slavery and who was their leader and law giver during their years of wandering in the wilderness he was from the family line of Levi he was also the brother of Aton and Miriam. Moses was a leader so inspired by God that he was able to build a race of oppressed and weary slaves.

Moses his faith confronts opposition and hostility by faith his parents hid him his life was saved he was a beautiful child they knew God had something great for the life of their child not scared of Pharaohs edict they kept him alive by their son's illustrious yes God reward faith just have it keep it you will be rewarded for it God will even prepare you tables in the presence of your enemies.

Don't be afraid of human and should maintain their separateness from the surroundings world just continue to worship and trust God and Keep the faith not letting nothing shakes your faith and stand on His word no weapon that's formagaist shall prosper. Faith will cause you to be triumph over your enemy's faith brings victory there are many who are in the bible we can talk about that had faith in God these are just some of the one's that was pick out by random Moses had to go before a king and tell Him to let the nation of Isreal go that was faith to to a king to tell the him to let go of people that he had in slavery for over 400 years it was by faith. That to step out of Egypt to Mount Sinai faith to lead that many people across the desert now it is important to have it and use it and put it into action when it is put into action things happen it don't take much the Bible said if you have faith the size of a mustard you can moved mountain don't know what your mountain is I know mine was the call mount witchcraft it was move to yonder place.

CHAPTER TWENTY

Love Your Enemies

The Bible said Luke.6: 27 and 35 But I say unto you which hear love your enemies do good to them which hate you. But Love ye your enemies and do good and lend hoping for nothing again and your reward shall be great and ye shall be the children of the Highest for he is kind. The unthankful and to the evil. Before we get any further first we must forgive we have to to forgive for the Father in heaven will forgive you if house unforgiveness you will do your self more harm then good it cause anger bitterness I hade to forgive and move on I had to release it forgetting those things that are behind me in order to move in to the things that God have for me while other move on you will be stuck spinning your wheels forgive so you can move on in the bible Matt. 5: 44 But I say unto you love enemies bless those who curse you do good to those who hate you and pray for those who spitefully use you and percure you. By having the love of God on the inside God is Love His Love will shine through us to love our enemies through by the Holy Spirit get flesh out of the way and let the love of Christ shine through. The best way to love your enemies is to follow the pattern of Jesus how he loves them He had plenty of them His love takes over in you you will be able to love your enemies and forgive them forgiveness is the act of excusing or pardoning others in spite of their slights short comming and errors farlhe more forgivess refers to God pardon of the sins of of human beings there is no other book on forgivness except the bible give us clear understanding that GOD 100% forgive sin.

If God forgive then we got to forgive one another. Keep moving in the love of Jesus Christ. His love will see you through it all as the old song said love lifted me when nothing else will help love lifted me don't make your enemies your haters make them your motivator.

CHAPTER TWENTY-ONE

Staying Focus on Love

Focus - The central point of attraction when God show you where you are going and what you are going to be doing stay focus in staying focus there will be a lot of distraction to get you off focus the enemy wants you off focus when Peter was walking on the water he was focusing on Jesus as he walk on the water when the storm caught his attenion he got off focus and began to sink as he going down he oh Lord save me Jesus reach out and lifted him up they both got into the boat the Bible said that we are not ignorant of the enemy devices distraction can come from various places it can come from family members Jona was told by God to go to Nineveh and preach to the city he got off focus paid the fare and went to Tarsha while he was on the boat and when a storm hit every man called on his God but Jonah knew that he was the problem for the storm so he told them to throw him over boad they did God had a prepared fish for Jona to be swallowed up Jonah he was in the belly for three days and night while in the belly he prayed and the fish swim to shore gurgytate Jonah up on land now Nineveh was a three day journey but he did it in one day it is important to stay focus on the Lord there are all kind of storm that can come up in life don't look at the storm but look at the one that control the storm Jesus is our great example on staying focus betrayed Jud and denied by Peter but

He stayed focus on what he came to do when Nehmia got word about Jerusalem how it was burned and the wall was down he went to the king the king gave him material to rebuild the walls as he was working on the walls his enemies came wanted him to come but he knew that they wanted to kill him and he told them I'm doing a great work and I can't come down when your doing a work for the Lord that when the enemy really will attack you and when God is getting ready to bless you that's when you will be attack by the devil Samson was the strongest man that ever lived.

He got off focus the Philistines ask Delilah to find out what was the secret to Samson strength she got him to take a nap in her lap he told her the secret to his strength if they cut the locks of his hair he would loose his strength. Samson had the Nazerite vow (I) no strong drink wine or liquor (2) not to shave their head (3) not come in contact with any thing that was dead she called them in and they cut the locks of his head she said Samson the Philistines are here he got up shook him self they got him put out his eyes out and they made sport of him he prayed to the God of Israel and the Lord to give him his strength and did it he between the two pillows the held up the stadium he killed more in his death then in his life time.

CHAPTER TWENTY-TWO

Love Lifted Me

There is a song that says love lifted me when nothing would help love lifted me God gave his Son and the Son gave His life.

Lifted - bring up to a higher position or place. Sometimes you can really go through that it can be a load on you it can make you feel low but come to realize that to feel low you are going to be raise up the beating of some trails can take its toll on you but to know that the Lord is with you for He on your side even the heat from the trail you will not affected by it when the hebrew boys was in the fire furnance they were in the furnance but they were not affected by it. His love will lift you up pass your pain your circumstance His love reaches on to the unreachable to the unlovable to the high and to the low no matter what or who you are His love his reaches out to you His love is real and genuine just keep on praising Him your praise confuse the enemy there was a man in the bible that had two sons and the younger one said Father give me portion of my inheritance and the Father gave it to him the young son left and went to a far country and wasted his living in that country he was brock out of money he got a job in the hog pin he look back home and thought about what His Father had back home and the love of God reach down in the hog pin lifted him up out of the hog pine no matter where you are the love of God is able to reach you the love of God reach the ·

young man and when he got home the Father said put a ring on his finger and shoes on his feet and a rob on him he once was lost but now he is found blind but now he sees the love of God got to the young man lifted him up out of the mud of the pin where the hogs was living but the love of God reach down in the mud got him clean him up and dress him up the smell of the hogs was on him but the love of Jesus His blood got rid of the smell of the hogs. In Matt and he said unto them what man shall have one sheep and if it falls into a pit on the Sabbath day.

On the Sabbath day will he not lay hold on it and lift it out here Jesus was talking to the Pharisees and they telling what unlawful to do on the Sabbath day it doesn't matter what day a day is the Love of JESUS is in the saving bussines in the book of Psalms 121 it said I will lift my eyes unto the hills from with commeth my help my help comes from the Lord which made the Heaven and the earth now that we know that JESUS will lift us up out of sin but we can lift Him up He said if I be lifted up from the earth I will draw all men unto me so lets lift our savior up.

CHAPTER TWENTY-THREE

Because God Loves Us

In the Bible in John 3:16 For GOD so love the world that He gave His only Begotten Son that whosoever believe in Him shall not perish but have Everlasting life.

God so love the world so is in the Greek (houtos) means what precedes or follows what follows is that He gave His only begotten Son.

His love toward mankind in the book of Titus 3:4 But after that the kindness and love of God our savior appeared when you read the first 3 verses it names a different thing for the flesh but get to verse 4 the Father shows His kindness and His love toward man kind matter how messed up we was He gave His love not the good that we done but by His mercy the mercy that end forth forever He loved us tenderly you a tender piece of steak taste you can soak your teeth into it not tough but it just much easier to chew and to handle that just how He gave His love to us no matter what we was His love and mercy was ther for the asking we just to accept it by the washing of the Spirit and the word and the rinsing of the Holy Spirit now there are 2 other things to this love we can receive it or reject it this love will proceed on us abundantly through JESUS CHRIST. To the cheerful 2cor 9:7 Every man according as he purposeth in his heart so let him give not grudgingly or of necessity for God loveth a cheerful giver not just be willing to give in the offerring but also be willing to give the praise willing to serve willing to read His word willing to give of one self.

The love of God is described as.

Great- Eph 2:4 But God is rich in mercy for his mercy for his great love where he loved us.

He is with love rich man or millionaire can fail for bankrupt but God never will have to fail bankrupt His love will at forever and not only His love goes beyond where a rich man money can go His love reach to the highest Mountain.

Great-- Abundant long many much plenteous.) Not only his love His love is great He Himself is great even the things is great.

Everlasting love - Jer 31:3 The Lord has appeared of old to me saying yes l have love you with an everlasting love therefore with loving kindness have I drawn you.

Sacrifical- Rom 5:8 But God commendeth his love toward us in that while we was yet sinners Christ died for us.

His love seen in the believers. Heart Rom SIS

Love- 1 Jolm 4:7-12
Faith--l John 4:16
Sercurity-2 Thessos 3:5
Daily life--1 John 4:15-17
Glorification-- 1 John 3: 1-2
CHRIST LOVE. Father- St. John 14:31
Believer--gal 2:20
Church-- eph, 5:2,25
Described as. KNOWING-- EPH.3:19
PERSONAL --Gal 2:20

CONQUERING-- ROM 8:37
UNBREAKABLE-- ROM8:35
IMITATIVE-- 1JOHN3:16
LIKE THE FATHER-- ST.JOHN 15:9
SACRIFICIAL- GAL 2:20

That's just how much that he loves us so my brothers and sisters in Christ JESUS God loves you and I do to may his love ever shine upon you.

CHAPTER TWENTY-FOUR

The Love of God Put My Life Back in Order

God is a God of order when something is out of order He speaks up about it not only lie is a God of order as Christians. He wants us to folllow His orders and also lie things done in order in the bible there was a man by the name of Noah in Gen. 6:8 But Noah found grace in the eyes of the Lord. These are the generation of Noah. Noah was a just man and perfect in his generation and walked with God. And Noah begat three sons ShcrnI lam and Japheth. The earth also was corrupt before God and the earth was filled with violence. And God looked upon the earth and behold it was corrupt for all flesh had corrupted his way upon the earth. And God said to Noah the end of all flesh is come before me for the earth is filled with violence through them and behold I will destroy them with the earth, make thee an ark of Copher wood rooms shall thou make in the ark and shall pitch it within and without with pitch. And this is the fashion which thou shall make it of the length of the ark shall be three hundred cubits the breath of it fifty cubits and the height of it shall be thiny cubits a window shall thou make to the ark and in a cubit shall thou finish it above and the door of the ark shall thou shall set in the side therefore with lower second and third stories shall thou make it.

And behold I even l do bring a flood of water upon the earth to destroy all flesh wherein is the breath of Iife from under heaven and everything that is in the earth shall die. But with thee will I establish my covenant and thou shall come into the ark thou and thy sons and thy wife and thy son's wives with thee. And of every living thing of all flesh two of every son shall thou bring into the ark to keep them alive with thee they shall be male and female. Of owls after their kind of every creeping thing of the earth after his kind two of every sort shall come unto thee to keep them alive. And take thou unto thee of all food that is eaten and thou shalt gather it to thee and it shall be for food for thee and for them. Thus did Noah according to all that God commanded him so did he. Noah followed the orders of God to the letter are you willing to follow God's orders and plan for your life the key is here that Noah obeyed God when you obey God you will obey God you will victorious. The bible said in the mist of the garden was the tree of good and evil God gave Adam the order not to touch it nor to eat from it the day you do you shall surely die Adam disobeyed God orders that why the 2nd Had to come and redeem man back to God.

Abraham followed God's orders in the book of Gen. 15:9 And He said Unto him take me an heifer of three years old and a she goat of three years old and Aram of three years old and a turtle dove and a young pigeon. And He took unto him all these and divided themin the mist and laid each piece one against another but the birds divided he not.

Verses 17 and 18 and it came to pass that when the sun went down and it was dark behold a smoking furnace and a burning lamp that passed between those pieces. In the same day the LORD made a covenant with Abram saying unto thy seed have I given this land from the river of Egypt unto the great river the river Euphrates. This is the Abrahamic covenant that God made with him and also a promise that God made him and that all male babies is to be circumcise covenant means - A coming together which signifies a mutual undertaking betwen two parties or more or more each binding himself to fulfill obligations for following God's orders GOD made him an promise that same promise goes for us today in Gal.3:29 And if ye be Christ's then are ye Abraham's seed and heirs according to the promise. In the book of Exodus Moses stood in the presence of God on Holy Ground God told him to pull off his shoes and God gave his orders to go to Egypt to tell Pharaoh to let His people go that they may come to the mountain and worship Him Moses did what love said for him to do 10 plagues was done but he let Israel gone followed God orders.

In the book of Exodus Love gave Moses orders how to build the tabernacle in the 25th chapter and the 9th verse on through the 26th chapter and the 27 The chapter God tell Moses that He wants Him where He wants him to do according to all that I show thereafter the pattern of the tabernacle and the pattern of all the instruments thereof even so shall ye make it. And they shall make an ark of shittim wood two cubit land a half shall be the lenth there of and a cubit and a half the breath thereof and cubit and a half the height thereof. And Moses goes on to follow God's order to the building of the tabernacle to the dressing of the Priests God gives the orders how He wants us to walk this Christian life by following His orders we can march right on through the tails of life.

In the bible we must follow the orders of God in the book of Deuteronomy The 28th chapter and it shall come to pass if thou shalt hearken diligently unto the voice of the Lord thy God to observe and to all His commmandments which I command thee this day that the Lord thy God will set thee on high above all nations of the earth. And all these blesing shall come on thee and overtake thee if thou shalt hearken unto the voice of the Lord thy God. If we will do this verses 3 to 15 talks about how and what God will do if we follow the orders that He have given if we don't follow the the orders verses 15 to 62 tell us what will happen to us if we are disobedient.

Gideon God gave orders to him the people that are with you

are to many in the book of Judges the 7th chapter they are to many for me to give the Medianites into there hands lest Isreal want to say thernselves against saying mine own hand hath saved me now Gideon did as God commanded Him first he said ye that is fearful and afraid let him return and depart early and twenty and two thousand left and there remained ten thousands and God said the people are yet to many bring them down unto the water I will try them for thee there and it shall be that of whom I say unto thee this shall go with thee and whomsoever I say unto thee this shall not go with thee the same shall not go so when they got down to the water the Lord said unto Gideon every one that lappeth of the water with his tongue as a dog lappeth him shah thou set by himself likewise every one that boweth down upon his knees to drink and the number of them that lapped putting their hand to their mouth were three hundred men but all the rest upon their knees so God told Gideon the three hundred men will deliver the Medianites into thine hands and he divided the men into three companies in every man hand he gave them ernpity pitchers and lamps within the pitchers and Gideon said blow the turn pets every man stood in his place they broke their pitchers they pursued after the Midianites and destroyed them.

As you can see God is a God of order we are to follow His orders as had said I top going to church God had to pull me into order first was my mind to be pull into idea love had to put my mind into his mind they was trying to control my mind I had to get the mind to start going back to church in the bible Philippians 2:5 Let this mind be in you which was also in Christ JESUS Romans 12:1-2 I beseech you therefore brethren by the mercies of God that ye present your bodies a living sacrifies holy acceptable unto God which is your reasonable service. And be not conformed to this world but be ye transformed by the renewing of your mind that ye may prove what is that good and acceptable and perfect will of God in 2Timothy 1:7 For God has not given us the spirit of fear but of power and of love and of a sound mind my mind had to be pull into place that I think the way that Christ want to think Christ is in control the love of Christ have complete control over my life and my mind love brought my mind back to order to think soberly the enemy will not have my mind the work of what I've been through trying to control my mind so God covers my mind in His blood now have the mind to go to church the bible said the God of this world has come to blind the mind of this world accept the gospel of light shine unto them.

Now the love and support of the saint praying for me my Father praying for me the spirit of oppression against my mind but God is in control of it all the bible says if we keep or mind on Him and He will keep us in perfect peace love pull my walk back with Him my steps are order by God.

As the song said walk in the light the beautiful light come wear the dew drops where mercy shine bright shin all around by day and by night Jesus the light of the world the just shall walk by faith and not by sight I walked in faith in our Lord and Savior Jeus Christ Enoch walked with God and had this testimony that he please God pleasing God is one of the impotant thing in a believers life what do you will not please everybody our goal is to please God in the bible the word of God said but they that wait on the Lord shall renew their strength they shall mound up with wings as an eagle they shall walk and not faint they shall run and not be weary. Because of what I been through and not going to church I mist out the annointing in the service now that the Lord put me back in order I got my joy back the joy of the Lord is my strength.

In getting my joy back I got my praise back I love to praise the Lord this joy the world didn't give it the world can't take it away joy means Hebrew word (chedvah) gladness, Greek (chairo) means to rejoice, gladness this joy is produced by the spirit of God the joy is unspeakable and to our sovereign God who workout all things for my ultimate good again the joy of the Lord is my strength. It a blessing to have joy even in the mist of a tail while you are going through it make the enemy and your enemies confuse that you still have the joy to make it through it may not feel good while you are going through it but to have the joy of the Lord on the inside give you that inner strength that no energy drink could not give you God is a good God oh last and see how good God is.

Peace I got my peace back in the book of Isaiah it said if you keep your mind on me that He would keep you in perfect peace whose mind is stayed on Him peace on the inside is an inner tranquility and poise of Christ because I trust in God. The peace that I got back Jesus spoke of it which is a combination of hope trust and quiet in the mind and soul brought about a connection to God.

Love gave me prayer life back I wasn't praying like should but love gave me my prayer life back and prayer time back it's a good feeling to have all night prayer again to get into the presence of God having all night prayer is always a blesing to me love put my prayer life together again the bible said men are to always pray and not faint.

Fasting love bless me to get back to fasting this only come through losing I am a person that love to fall and pray through fasting and praying is what help me to make it fasting loose the the bonds of wickedness undo the heavy burden of witchcraft off me through falling I started to going back to church the bible said don't forget to assemble yourself together by being with the saint Lord God for prayer and encouragement.

Reading the word of God and studying the word of God and listening to the word of God I knew that there is a higher calling on my life I'm in God's word to stay I'm planning to go back to bible college.

I love God so the love that save me is the love of the true and living God.

His Love is so real it picks me up when I was down I praise Him for that.

The love that He have for me His love in me and He loving me and I'm loving Him back oh what a love between my Lord and I God's love put everything in to order in my life my mind he put in order I'm lost in the love of Christ love have place my life back into order I'm blessed of the Lord and the great things He have done in my life truly I have come to understand that of what the word of God says the blessing of the Lord maketh thee rich and addeth no sorrow love have put all in order in my life the greatest thing that love has done on July 5th 2014 I meet the most incredible woman of my dreams a gorgeous woman by the name Diana. I tell you that love gave me greater when I meet Diana. I looked into her the most amazing eyes that I ever seen we was introducing we traded phone number yes it was love at first sight for me we started out a prayer partners praying over the phone I love her spirit and the more we prayed we got closer i knew that I wanted to spend the rest of my life with Diana. Now I know what love is and what love feel like God gave me the cream of the crop she is the most wonderful amazing woman in the world she is my inspiration my prayer partner she lift me up in prayer constantly. She completes me I prayed and ask the Lord to pick me a wife and He did. He looked in the city of Daytona Florida and bless me. I'm the happiest man in the world when God bless me with Diana. He gave me greater she loves the Lord. Love have pull my life together now we getting to get our first home together and many more other things that the Lord is going to bless us with on April 25th 2015 we got married beautiful wedding the Lord truly bless that day I say to you trust God and the love of God will see you through it all I can say love save me and the same love of our Lord and savior Jesus Christ will do the same for you in the bible it says in Eph. 3:20:

Now unto Him that is able to do exceeding abundantly above all that we ask or think according to the power that worketh in us His love will save you it did me when nothing else will help Love lifted me may God bless you and keep you is my prayer and you can always count on His Love.

CPSIA information can be obtained
at www.ICGtesting.com
Printed in the USA
BVHW041524300322
632755BV00010B/1086